MARILYN Norma Jeane

MARILYN *Norma Jeane*

TEXT BY GLORIA STEINEM
PHOTOGRAPHS BY GEORGE BARRIS

PENGUIN BOOKS

Penguin Books Ltd, 27 Wrights Lane, London W8 5TZ (Publishing and Editorial)
and Harmondsworth, Middlesex, England (Distribution and Warehouse)
Viking Penguin Inc., 40 West 23rd Street, New York, New York 10010, USA
Penguin Books Australia Ltd, Ringwood, Victoria, Australia
Penguin Books Canada Ltd, 2801 John Street, Markham, Ontario, Canada L3R 1B4
Penguin Books (NZ) Ltd, 182–190 Wairau Road, Auckland 10, New Zealand

First published in the USA by Henry Holt and Co., Inc., New York, 1986
Published in Penguin Books 1987

The publisher gratefully acknowledges permission to reprint excerpts from:
My Story by Marilyn Monroe, copyright © 1974 by Milton H. Greene, reprinted by permission of
Stein & Day Publishers.
Legend: The Life and Death of Marilyn Monroe by Fred Lawrence Guiles, copyright © 1984 by Fred Lawrence
Guiles, reprinted by permission of Stein & Day Publishers.
Marilyn Monroe Confidential by Lena Pepitone, William Stadiem, and Maurice Hakim, copyright © 1979 by Lena
Pepitone, William Stadiem, and Maurice Hakim, reprinted by permission of Simon & Schuster, Inc.
Your Inner Child of the Past by W. Hugh Missildine, copyright © 1963 by W. Hugh Missildine, reprinted by
permission of Simon & Schuster, Inc.
Goddess: The Secret Lives of Marilyn Monroe by Anthony Summers, copyright © 1985 by Anthony Summers,
reprinted by permission of Macmillan Publishing Company.

Portions of the last chapter have appeared in somewhat different form in *Ms.* magazine.

Made and printed in the U.S. by W. A. Krueger Co.

This book is dedicated to the real Marilyn. And to the reality in us all.

—Gloria Steinem

To a gentle, fragile Marilyn who will forever be in our hearts. Thanks for your friendship.

—George Barris

Contents

MARILYN *Norma Jeane*

This book began when George Barris, an American free-lance photojournalist, who had been living in Paris for more than twenty years, decided to publish the many photographs he had taken of Marilyn Monroe in June and July 1962 in California. They were probably the last ever taken of her alive.

Together with a text for which he had completed only one long interview, they were to become a book, an illustrated biography that would, in Marilyn's words, "set the record straight"; but this collaboration that she began on June 1, her thirty-sixth birthday, was never finished. Some of the photographs and quotes were used in newspaper reports after her death, but the book had been a joint project. George lost heart for it. In order to put some distance between himself and the sad sensationalism that followed her death, he moved to Paris. Once there, he met and married a French actress, Sylvie Constantine, became the father of two daughters who grew up there, and simply didn't come back. Over the years, some individual photos from those sessions were published, but most were not. Not until the approach of the twenty-fifth anniversary of Marilyn Monroe's death did he revisit the original idea of a book.

I owe my part in it to Dick Seaver, president of Henry Holt and Company, who was looking for a writer to help explain Marilyn as an individual and as an icon of continuing power. Certainly, our new understanding of who women are has increased our fascination with who Marilyn might have been. The goal of this project, therefore, could and should be closer to that of feminism in general: to include the viewpoints and influence of both women and men, and thus to have a better chance of seeing one woman's life as a whole. When Dick Seaver introduced me to George Barris, a gentle man who had been touched by Marilyn's willingness to open a part of her life to him, as well as by the loss of her magical presence, I think we both recognized in each other an empathy for our subject.

Because this was the first time I had ever written a text to accompany photographs, I had one extra writerly hope. I wanted to find a way to give words some of the nonlinear pleasure that images have always had. After all, each photograph is complete and enjoyable in itself. It can make sense on its own, whether we look at just that one, or go through a collection back to front, or start in the middle, or just browse; yet many photos taken of one subject can still

Facing page: George Barris photographs Marilyn in a borrowed house, in the summer of 1962, for the book that was to be their mutual project. Though she was living in her own home, the first and last she would ever own, it was still being renovated.

create a holograph in our mind's eye. That's why I have tried to write each chapter as an essay complete in itself. You may read about one aspect of Marilyn's life that you feel connected to or curious about, or choose several, or proceed in reverse, or read straight through as in a conventional book (for there is also some chronology to the order of chapters). But hopefully, you will find a microcosm of Marilyn's life in any one essay, and major themes will be repeated from different viewpoints in several essays, so that a factual and emotional holograph of a real person will begin to emerge.

George Barris and I shared one more idea: that this book might continue something that Marilyn herself cared about. When we discussed it, we realized that this "something" was clearly children—especially children who, like Marilyn as a child, needed more help, love, and protection than their own families could give. Almost everyone who saw Marilyn anywhere near children has remarked on the direct, emotional connection she had with them. Both at the times she did and at the times she did not want children of her own, she remained loyal and protective toward the children of her friends, and got special satisfaction from giving to an orphanage like the one where she had felt abandoned. Probably, she would have contributed more if she had paid attention to money or received a substantial percentage of the estimated $100 million that her films had earned when she died in 1962. (As a contract player, Marilyn received no more than $1,500 a week even when she was a big star, while other actresses who were her costars—for instance, Jane Russell in *Gentlemen Prefer Blondes*—might receive five or six times more. The largest single sum mentioned in Marilyn's will was only a $100,000 trust fund, part of which went to support Marilyn's institutionalized mother.)

For many of us whose lives coincided with Marilyn's, in reality or as a public image, her influence stretches both forward and backward.

For George Barris, this book began even before the taking of the photographs, or his current decision to publish them. It goes back to the fall of 1954, when he was assigned to photograph Marilyn Monroe while she filmed *The Seven Year Itch*. He stood with New York crowds as she was directed by Billy Wilder to repeat over and over again the famous scene in which air from a subway grating blows her white skirt high over her head, with the camera's eye inches away from her skin. ("I hope this isn't for your private collection, to be shown in stag shows," Barris remembered her saying to Wilder. Later, when the most provocative shots were not in the finished movie, George wondered if she might have been right.) Standing with Walter Winchell was Marilyn's then husband, Joe DiMaggio. When he could take the scene no more, DiMaggio just left. At a thank-you party Marilyn gave several days later for the cast and friends of the movie, George sat with her as she tried to track down Joe by phone, and talked tearfully about how lonely she was. It was the beginning of a friendship that was peripheral for Marilyn, but affected the course of George's life. Indeed, when he brought his family back to California to live, the first thing his two teenage daughters, Caroline and Stephanie, wanted to see was "where Marilyn was." He took them on a pilgrimage to Westwood Memorial Park, where Marilyn's body rests in a wall crypt; she did not wish to be buried.

For me, this book began when, in 1953, as a teenager who loved all movies, I still walked out of *Gentlemen Prefer Blondes* in embarrassment at seeing this whispering, simpering, big-breasted child-woman who was simply hoping her way into total vulnerability. How dare she be just as vulnerable and unconfident as I felt? Three years later, I went briefly to the Actors Studio, where confident New York actors seemed to take pleasure in ignoring this great, powerful, unconfident movie star who had dared to come to learn. She sat by herself, her body hidden in a shapeless black sweater and slacks, her skin luminescent as she put her hands up to her face, as if trying to hide herself, and she gradually became a presence in the room, if only because the rest of the group was trying so hard *not* to look at her. I remember feeling protective toward this famous woman who was older and more experienced than I; a protectiveness explained by the endlessly vulnerable child who looked out of Marilyn's eyes.

Wherever possible I have used her own words in this book. In addition to her interview with George Barris, I have quoted her from many sources, including her own unfinished autobiography, *My Story*, published from a manuscript she gave to business partner and friend Milton Greene. The confusing facts and stories of her early life were best researched by Fred Lawrence Guiles in *Legend: The Life and Death of Marilyn Monroe*. I owe a special thanks to Anthony Summers, whose 1985 book, *Goddess: The Secret Lives of Marilyn Monroe*, not only brought together existing research on her later life and the speculation surrounding her death, but also included many new interviews about those last months. Unless otherwise stated, the references in the latter half of "Fathers and Lovers" are largely taken from Summers's research.

In fact, so much has been reported about Marilyn Monroe in more than forty books written over the years that details of her life become colored pieces of glass in a kaleidoscope. If you read enough and turn them over enough, they fall into a pattern. (For instance, in one book, you learn that there was emerald jewelry in the toe of a slipper found in her closet by her last housekeeper. In another book, you learn that Frank Sinatra once gave her emerald earrings, and feel the joy of a detective.) The interviews I did myself served to confirm the

patterns that emerged, or to add some character-revealing anecdote. I am grateful to my friend Nancy Wartik of *Ms.* magazine, for fact-checking the pieces of that kaleidoscope, and to Catherine Fallin at Henry Holt, for editing and orchestrating this book's production.

There are also collectors of Monroe memorabilia who have put great time and effort into figuring out whether or not a woman in an old photograph was really Ana Lower, the woman Marilyn lived with as a teenager, or in what year a particular baby photograph must have been taken. I am especially indebted to the generosity of George Zeno, an expert who helped by giving us childhood and other photographs too early to be provided by George Barris, and so allowed us to see some of the people spoken about in Marilyn's early life.

I also thank the many people who shared their feelings about Marilyn Monroe with me, and who helped explain why her legend lasts and keeps its power.

Now, almost twenty-five years after her death, I notice the same phenomenon that was true when I first wrote a brief essay about Marilyn Monroe fifteen years ago: many of us remember the precise moment on August 5, 1962, when we first heard of her death. We remember where we were, what the room looked like, who was there. It's a sense memory usually reserved for the death of a president like Roosevelt or Kennedy, or a great leader like Martin Luther King, or a member of our own family. Even for those of us who are not old enough to have such a memory, her name is almost as familiar as that of the famous who are living now.

Her terrible openness made a connection with strangers. It seems never to end.

A special fund, the Marilyn Monroe Children's Fund, has been created with the Tavistock Clinic Foundation to help children in need. If you would like to contribute to this fund, send your donation to the Tavistock Clinic Foundation (marked 'Marilyn Monroe Children's Fund'), 120 Belsize Lane, London NW3 5BA, England. Another fund has been created in the U.S.A. of which my writer's fee for this book, a portion of George Barris's royalties, and a portion of the American publisher's profits make up the initial fund. Together, we can help Marilyn to help other children in the future.

THE WOMAN WHO WILL NOT DIE

I knew I belonged to the public and to the world, not because I was talented or even beautiful but because I had never belonged to anything or anyone else.

—from the unfinished autobiography of Marilyn Monroe

It has been nearly a quarter of a century since the death of a minor American actress named Marilyn Monroe. There is no reason for her to be part of my consciousness as I walk down a midtown New York street filled with color and action and life.

In a shop window display of white summer dresses, I see several huge photographs—a life-size cutout of Marilyn standing in a white halter dress, some close-ups of her vulnerable, please-love-me smile—but they don't look dated. Oddly, Marilyn seems to be just as much a part of this street scene as the neighboring images of models who could now be her daughters—even her granddaughters.

I walk another block and pass a record store featuring the hit albums of a rock star named Madonna. She has imitated Marilyn Monroe's hair, style, and clothes, but subtracted her vulnerability. Instead of using seduction to offer men whatever they want, Madonna uses it to get what she wants—a 1980s difference that has made her the idol of teenage girls. Nevertheless, her international symbols of femaleness are pure Marilyn.

A few doors away, a bookstore displays two volumes on Marilyn Monroe in its well-stocked window. The first is nothing but random photographs, one of many such collections that have been published over the years. The second is one of several recent exposés on the circumstances surrounding Monroe's 1962 death from an accidental or purposeful overdose of sleeping pills. Could organized crime, Jimmy Hoffa in particular, have planned to use her friendship with the Kennedys and her suicide—could Hoffa or his friends even have caused that suicide—in order to embarrass or blackmail Robert Kennedy, who was definitely a Mafia enemy and probably her lover? Only a few months ago, Marilyn Monroe's name made international headlines again when a British television documentary on this conspiracy theory was shown and a network documentary made in the United States was suppressed, with potential pressure from crime-controlled unions or from the late Robert Kennedy's family as rumored reasons.

As I turn the corner into my neighborhood, I pass a newsstand where the face of one more young Marilyn Monroe look-alike stares up at me from a glossy magazine cover. She is Kate

Facing page: Her image and name are still a multinational business. These samples are from the Sixth Annual Marilyn Monroe Memorabilia Show and Sale at Twentieth Century Antiques & Gallery, New York City. It is held from June 1 to August 5, the anniversary of her birth to that of her death.

Released in June 1955, this movie put a giant Marilyn on marquees around the world, and made that pose her most famous. *Facing page:* George Barris, a photojournalist on assignment, caught New York sidewalk crowds cheering as director Billy Wilder shot this scene over and over again, and Marilyn's then husband, Joe DiMaggio, did a slow burn on the sidelines.

Mailer, Norman Mailer's daughter, who was born the year that Marilyn Monroe died. Now she is starring in *Strawhead*, a "memory play" about Monroe written by Norman Mailer, who is so obsessed with this long-dead sex goddess that he had written one long biography and another work—half fact, half fiction—about her, even before casting his daughter in this part.

The next morning, I turn on the television and see a promotion for a show on film director Billy Wilder. The only clip chosen to attract viewers and represent Wilder's entire career is one of Marilyn Monroe singing a few breathless bars in *Some Like It Hot*, one of two films they made together.

These are everyday signs of a unique longevity. If you add her years of movie stardom to the years since her death, Marilyn Monroe has been part of our lives and imaginations for nearly four decades. That's a very long time for one celebrity to survive in a throwaway culture.

In the 1930s, when English critic Cyril Connolly proposed a definition of posterity to measure whether a writer's work had stood the test of time, he suggested that posterity should be limited to ten years. The form and content of popular culture were changing too fast, he explained, to make any artist accountable for more than a decade.

Since then, the pace of change has been accelerated even more. Everything from the communications revolution to multinational entertainment has altered the form of culture. Its content has been transformed by civil rights, feminism, an end to film censorship, and much more. Nonetheless, Monroe's personal and intimate ability to inhabit our fantasies has gone right on. As I write this, she is still better known than most living movie stars, most world leaders, and most television personalities. The surprise is that she rarely has been taken seriously enough to ask why that is so.

One simple reason for her life story's endurance is the premature end of it. Personalities and narratives projected onto the screen of our imaginations are far more haunting—and far more likely to be the stuff of conspiracies and conjecture—if they have not been allowed to play themselves out to their logical or illogical ends. James Dean's brief life is the subject of a cult, but the completed lives of such similar "outsiders" as Gary Cooper or Henry Fonda are not. Each day in the brief Camelot of John Kennedy inspires as much speculation as each year in the long New Deal of Franklin Roosevelt. The few years of Charlie "Bird" Parker's music inspire graffiti ("Bird Lives"), but the many musical years of Duke Ellington do not.

When the past dies, there is mourning, but when the future dies our imaginations are compelled to carry it on.

Would Marilyn Monroe have become the serious actress she aspired to be? Could she have survived the transition from sex goddess to mortal woman that aging would impose? Could she have stopped her disastrous marriages to men whose images she wanted to absorb (Beloved American DiMaggio, Serious Intellectual Miller), and found a partner who loved and understood her as she really was? Could she have kicked her life-wasting habits of addiction and procrastination? Would she have had or adopted children? Found support in the growing strength of women or been threatened by it? Entered the world of learning or continued to be ridiculed for trying? Survived and even enjoyed the age of sixty she now would be?

Most important, could she finally have escaped her lifetime combination of two parts talent, one part victim, and one part joke? Would she have been "taken seriously," as she so badly wanted to be?

We will never know. Every question is as haunting as any of its possible answers.

But the poignancy of this incompleteness is not enough to explain Marilyn Monroe's enduring power. Even among brief public lives, few become parables. Those that endure seem to hook into our deepest emotions of hope or fear, dream or nightmare of what our own fates might be. Successful leaders also fall into one group or the other: those who invoke a threatening future and promise disaster unless we obey, and those who conjure up a hopeful future and promise reward if we will follow. It's this power of either fear or hope that makes a personal legend survive, from the fearsome extreme of Adolf Hitler (Did he really escape? Might he have lived on in the jungles of South America?) to the hopeful myth of Zapata waiting in the hills of Mexico to rescue his people. The same is true for the enduring fictions of popular culture, from the frightening villain to the hopeful hero, each of whom is reincarnated again and again.

In an intimate way during her brief life, Marilyn Monroe hooked into both those extremes of emotion. She personified many of the secret hopes of men and many secret fears of women.

To men, wrote Norman Mailer, her image was "gorgeous, forgiving, humorous, compliant and tender . . . she would ask no price." She was the child-woman who offered pleasure without adult challenge; a lover who neither judged nor asked anything in return. Both the roles she played and her own public image embodied a masculine hope for a woman who is innocent and sensuously experienced at the same time. "In fact," as Marilyn said toward the end of her career, "my popularity seemed almost entirely a masculine phenomenon."

Since most men have experienced female power only in their childhoods, they associate it with a time when they themselves were powerless. This will continue as long as children are raised almost totally by women, and rarely see women in authority outside the home. That's why male adults, and some females too, experience the presence of a strong woman as a dangerous regression to a time of their own vulnerability and dependence. For men, especially, who are trained to measure manhood and maturity by their distance from the world of women, being forced back to that world for female companionship may be very threatening indeed. A compliant child-woman like Monroe solves this dilemma by offering sex *without* the power of an adult woman, much less of an equal. As a child herself, she allows men to feel both conquering and protective; to be both dominating and admirable at the same time.

For women, Monroe embodied kinds of fear that were just as basic as the hope she offered men: the fear of a sexual competitor who could take away men on whom women's identities and even livelihoods might depend; the fear of having to meet her impossible standard of always giving—and asking nothing in return; the nagging fear that we might share her feminine fate of being vulnerable, unserious, constantly in danger of becoming a victim.

Aside from her beautiful face, which women envied, she was nothing like the female stars that women moviegoers have made popular. Those stars offered at least the illusion of being in control of their fates—and perhaps having an effect on the world. Stars of the classic "women's movies" were actresses like Bette Davis, who made her impact by sheer force of emotion; or Katharine Hepburn, who was always intelligent and never victimized for long; or even Doris Day, who charmed the world into conforming to her own virginal standards. Their figures were admirable and neat, but without the vulnerability of the big-breasted woman in a society that regresses men and keeps them obsessed with the maternal symbols of breasts and hips.

Watching Monroe was quite different: women were forced to worry about her vulnerability—and thus their own. They might feel like a black moviegoer watching a black actor play a role that was too passive, too obedient, or a Jew watching a Jewish character who was selfish and avaricious. In spite of some extra magic, some face-saving sincerity and humor, Marilyn Monroe was still close to the humiliating stereotype of a dumb blonde: depersonalized, sexual, even a joke. Though few women yet had the self-respect to object on behalf of their sex, as one would object on behalf of a race or religion, they still might be left feeling a little humiliated—or threatened—without knowing why.

"I have always had a talent for irritating women since I was fourteen," Marilyn wrote in her unfinished autobiography. "Sometimes I've been to a party where no one spoke to me for a whole evening. The men, frightened by their wives or sweeties, would give me a wide berth. And the ladies would gang up in a corner to discuss my dangerous character."

But all that was before her death and the revelations surrounding it. The moment she was gone, Monroe's vulnerability was no longer just a turn-on for many men and an embarrassment for many women. It was a tragedy. Whether that final overdose was suicide or not, both men and women were forced to recognize the insecurity and private terrors that had caused her to attempt suicide several times before.

Men who had never known her wondered if their love and protection might have saved her. Women who had never known her wondered if their empathy and friendship might have done the same. For both women and men, the ghost of Marilyn came to embody a particularly powerful form of hope: the rescue fantasy. Not only did we imagine a happier ending for the parable of Marilyn Monroe's life, but we also fantasized ourselves as the saviors who could have brought it about.

Still, women didn't seem quite as comfortable about going public with their rescue

1954: Crowds gathered outside the East Sixties brownstone in Manhattan, watching a scene of Marilyn leaning out the window to call to costar Tom Ewell. When she turned to find Barris photographing, she said cheerfully, "I hope you got some good shots of my tush."

fantasies as men did. It meant admitting an identity with a woman who always had been a little embarrassing, and who had now turned out to be doomed as well. Nearly all of the journalistic eulogies that followed Monroe's death were written by men. So are almost all of the more than forty books that have been published about Monroe.

Bias in the minds of editors played a role, too. Consciously or not, they seemed to assume that only male journalists should write about a sex goddess. Margaret Parton, a reporter for the *Ladies' Home Journal* and one of the few women assigned to profile Marilyn during her lifetime, wrote an article that was rejected because it was too favorable. She had reported Marilyn's ambitious hope of playing Sadie Thompson, under the guidance of Lee Strasberg, in a television version of "Rain," based on a short story by Somerset Maugham. (Sadie Thompson was "a girl who knew how to be gay, even when she was sad," a fragile Marilyn had explained, "and that's important—you know?") Parton also reported her own "sense of having met a sick little canary instead of a peacock. Only when you pick it up in your hand to comfort it . . . beneath the sickness, the weakness and the innocence, you find a strong bone structure, and a heart beating. You *recognize* sickness, and you *find* strength."

Whitey Snyder, Marilyn's make-up man, lifts her up for Barris's photographs in the summer of 1962. Nine years earlier, when she was working on *Gentlemen Prefer Blondes,* Marilyn had given Snyder a gold clip inscribed, "While I'm Still Warm, Marilyn."

Bruce and Beatrice Gould, editors of the *Ladies' Home Journal,* told Parton she must have been "mesmerized" to write something so uncritical. "If you were a man," Mr. Gould told her, "I'd wonder what went on that afternoon in Marilyn's apartment." Fred Guiles, one of Marilyn Monroe's more fair-minded biographers, counted the suppression of this sensitive article as one proof that many editors were interested in portraying Monroe, at least in those later years, as "crazy, a home wrecker."

Just after Monroe's death, one of the few women to write with empathy was Diana Trilling, an author confident enough not to worry about being trivialized by association—and respected enough to get published. Trilling regretted the public's "mockery of [Marilyn's] wish to be educated," and her dependence on sexual artifice that must have left "a great emptiness where a true sexuality would have supplied her with a sense of herself as a person." She mourned Marilyn's lack of friends, "especially women, to whose protectiveness her extreme vulnerability spoke so directly."

"But we were the friends," as Trilling said sadly, "of whom she knew nothing."

In fact, the contagion of feminism that followed Monroe's death by less than a decade may be the newest and most powerful reason for the continuing strength of her legend. As women began to be honest in public, and to discover that many of our experiences were more societal than individual, we also realized that we could benefit more by acting together than

by deserting each other. We were less likely to blame or be the victim, whether Marilyn or ourselves, and more likely to rescue ourselves and each other.

In 1972, the tenth anniversary of her death and the birth year of *Ms.*, the first magazine to be published by and for women, Harriet Lyons, one of its early editors, suggested that *Ms.* do a cover story about Marilyn called "The Woman Who Died Too Soon." As the writer of this brief essay about women's new hope of reclaiming Marilyn, I was astounded by the response to the article. It was like tapping an underground river of interest. For instance:

Marilyn had talked about being sexually assaulted as a child, though many of her biographers had not believed her. Women wrote in to tell their similar stories. It was my first intimation of what since has become a documented statistic: One in six adult women has been sexually assaulted in childhood by a family member. The long-lasting effects—for instance, feeling one has no value except a sexual one—seemed shared by these women and by Marilyn. Yet most were made to feel guilty and alone, and many were as disbelieved by the grown-ups around them as Marilyn had been.

Physicians had been more likely to prescribe sleeping pills and tranquilizers than to look for the cause of Monroe's sleeplessness and anxiety. They had continued to do so even after she had attempted suicide several times. Women responded with their own stories of being overmedicated, and of doctors who assumed women's physical symptoms were "all in their

Following pages: 1962: Marilyn asked George Barris to buy props, this sweater and towels among them, for the beach shots in their book, which was one of her last projects.

minds." It was my first understanding that women are more likely to be given chemical and other arm's-length treatment, and to suffer from the assumption that they can be chemically calmed or sedated with less penalty because they are doing only "women's work." Then, ads in medical journals blatantly recommended tranquilizers for depressed housewives, and even now, the majority of all tranquilizer prescriptions are written for women.

Acting, modeling, making a living more from external appearance than from internal identity—these had been Marilyn's lifelines out of poverty and obscurity. Other women who had suppressed their internal selves to become interchangeable "pretty girls"—and as a result were struggling with both lack of identity and terror of aging—wrote to tell their stories.

To gain the seriousness and respect that was largely denied her, and to gain the fatherly protection she had been completely denied, Marilyn married a beloved American folk hero and then a respected intellectual. Other women who had tried to marry for protection or for identity, as women often are encouraged to do, wrote to say how impossible and childlike this had been for them, and how impossible for the husbands who were expected to provide their wives' identities. But Marilyn did not live long enough to see a time in which women sought their own identities, not just derived ones.

During her marriage to Arthur Miller, Marilyn had tried to have a child—but suffered an ectopic pregnancy, a miscarriage—and could not. Letters poured in from women who also suffered from this inability and from a definition of womanhood so tied to the accident of the physical ability to bear a child—preferably a son, as Marilyn often said, though later she also talked of a daughter—that their whole sense of self had been undermined. "Manhood means many things," as one reader explained, "but womanhood means only one." And where is the self-respect of a woman who wants to give birth only to a male child, someone different from herself?

Most of all, women readers mourned that Marilyn had lived and died in an era when there

were so few ways for her to know that these experiences were shared with other women, that she was not alone.

Now women and men bring the past quarter century of change and understanding to these poignant photographs taken in the days just before her death. It makes them all the more haunting.

I still see the self-consciousness with which she posed for a camera. It makes me remember my own teenage discomfort at seeing her on the screen, mincing and whispering and simply hoping her way into love and approval. By holding a mirror to the exaggerated ways in which female human beings are trained to act, she could be as embarrassing—and as sad and revealing—as a female impersonator.

Yet now I also see the why of it, and the woman behind the mask that her self-consciousness creates.

I still feel worried about her, just as I did then. There is something especially vulnerable about big-breasted women in this world concerned with such bodies, but unconcerned with the real person within. We may envy these women a little, yet we feel protective of them, too.

But in these photographs, the body emphasis seems more the habit of some former self. It's her face we look at. Now that we know the end of her story, it's the real woman we hope to find—looking out of the eyes of Marilyn.

In the last interview before her death, close to the time of these photographs, Patricia Newcomb, her friend and press secretary, remembers that Marilyn pleaded unsuccessfully with the reporter to end his article like this:

> What I really want to say: That what the world really needs is a real feeling of kinship. Everybody: stars, laborers, Negroes, Jews, Arabs. We are all brothers.
> Please don't make me a joke. End the interview with what I believe.

You could buy a sackful of old bread . . . for twenty-five cents. Aunt Grace and I would stand in line for hours waiting to fill our sack. When I looked up at her, she would grin at me and say, "Don't worry, Norma Jeane. You're going to be a beautiful girl when you grow up. I can feel it in my bones."

—*from the unfinished autobiography of Marilyn Monroe*

One cloudy Sunday in 1962, Marilyn Monroe sat down for an interview with photojournalist George Barris in the patio of her house in Brentwood, California. Wrapped in a light blue terry-cloth robe and sipping champagne, she was about to supply the personal text for the photographic book that was to be their mutual project that summer. She wanted to set the record straight.

"Lies, lies, lies, everything they've been saying about me is lies," she said sadly. "This is the first true story; you're the first one I've told it to," she insisted to Barris, as she had to others. "I'll tell you all about my childhood, career, marriages and divorces, and what I want out of life." Just as Marilyn seemed to have told more than one man that her first sexual pleasure had been with him, she also offered her life to reporters whom she liked. It was one of the many small ways she sought approval.

But on this day, there was an added motive. The "lies" she referred to were news reports that she was depressed, suffering from deep feelings of inferiority, and incapable of working. Having been fired from a Hollywood sex comedy called *Something's Got to Give* for lateness, absence, illness, and a spaciness that rendered unusable even some of the footage she did finish, she was now fighting for her professional life. "My work is the only ground I've ever had to stand on," she had told a magazine writer that final summer. "To put it bluntly, I seem to be a whole superstructure with no foundation. But I'm working on the foundation."

Now Marilyn was using this interview to tell Hollywood she was not "unemployable." She was putting up a cheerful front. "I am not a victim of emotional conflicts," she protested to Barris. "I'm human, we all have our areas, we all feel a little inferior, but who ever admits it?"

Settling into a wicker chair with her champagne glass in hand, she began to respond to questions—and also to tell a familiar story.

"Yes, it's true I was born an illegitimate child," she began, tucking her bare feet underneath her. To Barris, she looked amazingly young and beautiful; a decade younger than the thirty-sixth birthday she had just celebrated. "I also spent most of my childhood in and out of foster

Facing page: André de Dienes, the photographer who fell in love with the nineteen-year-old Norma Jeane on a long modeling trip, and photographed her throughout her life, took this photo on a beach near New York, in 1949.

homes, and to top it off I landed in an orphanage, even though my mother was and still is alive.

"My father never married my mother," she went on. "I guess that's what broke her heart. . . . When you love a man and tell him you're going to have his child and he runs out on you, it's something a woman never gets over. I don't think my mother ever did. . . .

"You know, my mother was a very attractive woman when she was young," she said proudly, digressing from a chronology that seemed to depress her. "But she used to tell me her mother—that was my grandmother Della Monroe—was the real beauty in the family. She came from Dublin, Ireland, where all the girls are pretty. My grandfather came from Scotland. I remember my mother spoke with a slight Scotch brogue, but it sounded nice, sort of musical. . . .

1928: Norma Jeane, boarded out since birth, on a rare outing with her mother Gladys.

"No, I never knew my father. My mother once told me he died in an accident when I was quite young. In fact, he left my mother when he heard from her that I was on the way. It must have hurt my mother very, very much. It could even drive some women out of their mind. . . . My mother had a nervous breakdown and had to be sent to the hospital for a rest when I was only five years old. That's what caused me to spend my childhood in and out of foster homes."

Marilyn put her champagne glass down and was silent. However familiar the story she was telling, the emotion of it was getting to her.

"What happened next in my life, I don't think I can ever forget," she said as if to herself. "My mother's best girlfriend at this time, Aunt Grace, was my legal guardian, and I was living in her home. But when she remarried all of a sudden, the house became too small, and someone had to go. . . . One day she packed my clothes and took me with her in her car. We drove and drove without her ever saying a word.

"When we came to a three-story red-brick building, she stopped the car and we walked up the stairs to the entrance. I saw this sign, and the emptiness that came over me, I'll never forget. The sign read: LOS ANGELES ORPHANS' HOME.

"I began to cry. 'Please, please don't make me go inside. I'm not an orphan, my mother's not dead. I'm not an orphan—it's just that she's sick in the hospital and can't take care of me. Please don't make me live in an orphans' home!'

"I was crying and protesting—I still remember they had to use force to drag me inside that place.

"I may have been only nine years old, but something like this, you never forget. The whole world around me just crumbled.

"I later learned that the day Aunt Grace had taken me to the orphans' home, she cried all morning. She also did promise me that as soon as she could, she would take me out of that place. She used to come and visit me often, but when a little girl feels lost and lonely and that nobody wants her, it's something she never can forget as long as she lives."

Marilyn had been in her own world, but now she suddenly returned. "I let him out so he could feel free to run around . . . but he's been so quiet, it's not like him . . . ," she said, looking around her.

It took Barris a few moments to understand that she was talking about her white poodle, Maf, a gift given to her by a woman friend so that Marilyn would have company when she emerged from hospital psychiatric treatment in New York a year before. Only when the small dog had been called from a corner of the garden and hugged with great affection did Marilyn settle down again.

"They say you soon forget the bad things in your life, and only remember the good ones," she continued, picking up her champagne glass_again. "Well, maybe for others it's that way, but not for me. . . .

"When I was about eight years old, I lived in this foster home that took in boarders. There was this old man they all would cater to, he was the star boarder. One day I was upstairs on the first floor where his room was, putting some towels in the hall linen closet. His door was open and he called me into the room. I went into the room, and he immediately bolted the door. He asked me to sit on his lap and he kissed me and started doing other things to me. He said, 'It's only a game!'

"He let me go when the game was over.

"When he unlocked the door, I ran to my foster mother and told her what he did to me.

1939: Norma Jeane at about thirteen with a woman who is thought to be Ana Lower (Aunt Ana) with whom Marilyn lived as a teenager.

She looked at me, shocked . . . then slapped me across the mouth and shouted at me, 'I don't believe you! Don't you dare say such things about that nice man!'

"I was so hurt, I began to stammer. She didn't believe me! I cried that night in bed all night, I just wanted to die. . . .

"This was the first time I can ever remember stammering. . . . Once afterward when I was in the orphanage, I started to stutter out of the clear blue. . . . There were odd times when I couldn't get a word out." And indeed, movie directors who worked with Marilyn had been surprised to find that she sometimes stuttered when she felt frightened or criticized.

Whatever Marilyn's intention of using this interview to show her control and good cheer, it was dissolving in the flood of childhood memories that seemed to wash away the years and turn her into Norma Jeane again. The two most painful and often told scenes—the eight-year-old Norma Jeane who was sexually attacked and then disbelieved, her abandonment to an orphanage a year or so later—had been reversed in the telling today, but they clearly were wounds that had not healed.

"My mother was committed to the Norwalk State Hospital," Marilyn said, resuming her narrative, "and she stayed there until I was nineteen. But Aunt Grace had made me a promise that someday she would take me out of the orphanage. When I was eleven, she kept her word. She had me released, but this time, I didn't go to live with her. She took me to a very poor neighborhood in an outlying section of Los Angeles. I was to live there with her aunt, a sixty-two-year-old spinster. The house was a run-down bungalow. The people in the neighborhood were mostly poor and on relief.

"I'll never forget living there, because she became my Aunt Ana. Her name was Miss Ana Lower, and she was the greatest influence on my whole life. She was the only person I ever loved with such a deep love that one can only have for someone so good, so kind, and so full of love for me.

"One of the many reasons I loved her so much was because of her philosophy . . . her understanding of what really mattered in life. Like the time when I was going to Emerson Junior High and one of the girls in my class made fun of a dress I was wearing. . . . I ran home crying as if my heart would break. My loving Aunt Ana just held me in her arms and rocked me to and fro like a baby and said, 'It doesn't make any difference if other children make fun of you, or of your clothes, or where you live. Always remember, dear: it's what you are that really counts. Just keep being yourself, honey, that's all that matters.'

"She didn't believe in sickness, disease, or death," Marilyn remembered of this gentle Christian Scientist who had been her protector. "She didn't believe in a person being a failure, either. She believed the mind could achieve anything it wished to achieve. I loved her with all my heart.

Facing page: Norma Jeane Dougherty at about eighteen. An arranged marriage was her only security.

"When I was married just after my sixteenth birthday, it was Aunt Ana who designed and made my wedding gown. I was so proud to be called her niece on my marriage certificate."

If this description of marriage seemed to come in the midst of childhood, that was also the way it had happened for Norma Jeane.

For one thing, her body had matured early. "I always looked older than my age," Marilyn explained. "When I was just ten years old, I shot up to my present height of five feet, five inches—except then I was skinny; I looked very boyish. When I was twelve years old, I may still have been a baby inside, but outside I had the body of a woman."

For another, Aunt Grace was moving away from Los Angeles with her new husband; Aunt Ana was considered too old to take her place as Norma Jeane's legal guardian; and an arranged marriage seemed the only alternative to another foster home or a return to the orphanage. "Again it was the case of not being wanted," Marilyn said slowly. "I remember Aunt Grace saying something about really being quite a mature woman, and it was time I thought of marriage. Of course, this frightened me. I protested, 'But I'm too young,' and her answer was, 'Only in years, only in years.' When I told Aunt Grace I was frightened of what a husband might do, she seemed quite surprised at my innocence."

The bridegroom Aunt Grace had in mind for Norma Jeane as soon as she could legally marry was Jim Dougherty, the almost twenty-one-year-old son of a neighbor family, and she suggested the match to his parents. "After we had gone out for several months, we got married on June nineteenth, nineteen forty-two," Marilyn said, remembering the exact date after all these years. "I was sweet sixteen on June first. We had a double-ring ceremony. My Aunt Ana bought me a book that contained the hints a bride-to-be should know. . . . I guess that even by today's standards, I'd be considered a child bride. You know, I had six mothers weeping when I marched down the aisle? I guess they all considered me their daughter, and in a way I was. They all were my foster mothers.

"Being married to Jim brought me escape at the time. It was that or being sent off to another foster home. . . . I've been told Jim has said I was a most responsive bride, a perfect bride in every respect except the cooking department.

"It was in nineteen forty-four that Jim enlisted in the merchant marine. After he had boot training, he was stationed at Catalina Island as a physical training instructor, and I was permitted to join him there. It was a world of men. . . . Besides sailors and their families, there were Marines, SeaBees, Coast Guardsmen, and not too many girls. . . . My husband always seemed jealous and annoyed when the men would whistle at me. He used to lecture me about the type of clothes I was wearing. Actually, I wore the same clothes the other girls wore. . . . I just couldn't understand him acting that way.

"When Jim was sent to Shanghai, I went back to Van Nuys and lived with his family. I was working then at the Radio Plane Company in Burbank. I had started there as a parachute inspector and now was promoted to the 'dope room.' I used to spray this liquid dope, which is made by mixing banana oil and glue, on the plane fuselages.

"Well, one day a photographer came to our plant from the Army's Pictorial Center in Hollywood to take some pictures of people—he called them morale-booster types—showing how they were doing their part, working in defense plants, too. When this photographer, David Conover, passed by where I was at work, he said, 'You're a real morale booster. I'm going to take your picture for the boys in the Army to keep their morale high.'

Jim Dougherty, Norma Jeane's first husband, with his young bride in 1944.

1945: Norma Jeane Dougherty metamorphoses into a model and hopeful starlet.

"First he took pictures of me in my overalls. When he discovered I had a sweater in my locker, he asked if I would mind wearing it for more pictures. 'I want to show the boys what you really look like,' he said.

"Those pictures he took of me were the first that ever appeared in a publication. They were used in hundreds of Army camp newspapers, including *Yank* and *Stars and Stripes*. When this Army photographer called me a few weeks later, he had shown them to a commercial photographer in Los Angeles.

"The photographer was Potter Hueth, and he told me I had that 'natural look.' . . . If I wanted to speculate with him, he would take pictures of me and when he sold them to the magazines, he would then pay me. The fee usually was five to ten dollars—a lot of money in those days. What did I have to lose? I agreed, providing I could do it at night and not lose time at the defense plant.

"Some of these pictures he showed to Miss Snively, who ran the largest modeling agency in Los Angeles. She told me I had the makings of a model, but that I would have to attend the modeling school she also operated so I could be properly groomed. The tuition was one hundred dollars. I told her, 'Well, that lets me out—I don't have the money.' She told me not to worry; I could pay this out of the modeling jobs she would get for me.

"I remember the first modeling job I ever had. I was hostess at an aluminum exhibit at the Los Angeles Home Show. . . . I received ten dollars a day for nine days, but all of it went for my modeling lessons. My second job turned out quite bad. A group of models went on location to Malibu Beach to model sports clothes for a famous American catalogue. After two days, they sent me home. They wouldn't tell me why, and I was upset—here I was, the only model fired.

"Later, I found out the reason. They said no one would ever look at the clothes in their catalogue. 'It's just that you have more than the usual amount of sex appeal. Too much to make a fashion model,' Miss Snively explained to me.

"They started to put me into bathing suits, and all of a sudden I became popular. Photographers liked working with me. They said I knew how to take direction. . . . I was a brunette then, and Miss Snively kept insisting I bleach my hair. I kept refusing. 'If you expect to go places, you've got to be a blonde,' she said. 'Photographers can photograph a blonde differently, light or dark and those in-between shades, by their control of lighting.' "

Norma Jeane stopped resisting this symbol of her changing self when a six-hour assignment for shampoo ads depended on it. "I couldn't get used to myself," Marilyn remembered, her platinum hair now turned to cotton candy by years of bleachings, "but it did bring me more modeling work. I was getting more and more assignments for glamour poses and cheesecake."

The young model Norma Jeane, hair not yet lightened or straightened as Marilyn, learns a standard smile.

The refuge once offered by her young husband had disappeared. In spite of her pleadings and her fear of being abandoned, even for a year or two, Jim Dougherty had joined the merchant marine. Now the sensual body that had brought a shy, frightened little girl such unexpected notice was becoming her only security and passport into another world. Her young husband had never understood her dreams. "Jim used to discourage me by saying, 'There are plenty of beautiful girls who can act and Hollywood's full of them; they're all looking for work. What makes you think you're any better than them?' I don't think he really knew how I felt inside.

"When my lawyer wrote to Jim in Shanghai about my wanting a divorce, Jim asked if I would wait until he returned from overseas to see if we could make a go of our marriage. It was then I knew more than ever I wanted to become an actress. Perhaps through modeling I could get the break I needed."

As Barris was scribbling in his notepad, dusk had fallen in the garden. Marilyn wrapped her blue terry-cloth robe more tightly around her and suggested they move indoors. She walked barefoot into the kitchen for more beer for him, more champagne for her, and was solicitous about his comfort in the small high-ceilinged living room with space for just a couch and two chairs. "Let's drink a toast to the future and what it holds in store for us," Marilyn proposed. They raised their glasses to each other before continuing.

"Things were really happening for me as a model," Marilyn explained. "I was appearing in all of the magazines of the day, especially the men's magazines. Howard Hughes, who was then the owner of RKO Studios, noticed me in those magazines, and asked his studio to do a screen test. Miss Snively called Ben Lyon, a talent scout at Twentieth Century-Fox. She called an agent named Helen Ainsworth to look after me, and the agent had also heard that Twentieth Century-Fox was looking for new faces.

"I'll never forget that first meeting with Mr. Lyon. He didn't ask if I had any experience, he didn't ask me to read scripts, but the fact that Mr. Hughes was interested for *his* studio was reason enough for him to see me. He said he wanted to give me a color screen test, but all the color tests had to be approved by Darryl Zanuck, who was head of production. He was out of town for some time, and I would have to wait until he returned.

"Miss Ainsworth turned to Mr. Lyon and said, 'If you don't give this girl a screen test, I'm going to take her over to that other [Howard Hughes's] studio right now.' I just sat there praying that nothing would go wrong.

"Two days later, Mr. Lyon authorized a color screen test for me. Mr. Leon Shamroy, the motion-picture cameraman who was the best, was to photograph me. There was a picture in production then called *Mother Wore Tights*, starring Betty Grable. Secretly, at five-thirty one morning, Mr. Lyon, Mr. Shamroy, and myself sneaked on the set. I made up in a portable dressing room, Mr. Lyon sneaked a sequined evening gown out of wardrobe, and Mr. Shamroy lighted the set himself and loaded his motion-picture camera himself.

"This is what my scene consisted of: I walked across the stage set, sat down, then I had to light a cigarette, put it out, go upstage, cross, look out the window, sit down, come downstage, and then exit," said Marilyn, remembering every detail of those first stage directions given to Norma Jeane sixteen years before. "Those bright lights were blinding. For some strange reason, instead of being nervous and scared, I just tried very hard because I knew Mr. Lyon and Mr. Shamroy were taking an awful chance. If it didn't work out well, they might get in trouble."

George Barris now told Marilyn something Shamroy had said about that session: "I got a cold chill. This girl had something I haven't seen since the days of silent pictures; this girl had sex on a piece of film like Jean Harlow had. Every frame of that film radiated sex. . . ."

The more confident Marilyn—the one who had tried to reject Hollywood's grade-B sex pictures and escape to acting lessons in New York—might have objected to that judgment. "I wanted to be an artist, not an erotic freak," she protested once. She had even taken on the studio system by starting her own production company.

But this later Marilyn was fighting to work at all, even in *Something's Got to Give*, the sex comedy in which she had little faith. She just accepted the description and walked around the room for a moment, lost in her own thoughts. "You know, it's strange how it only seems yesterday," she said, returning to her chair. "It's amazing how much of the past a person's mind has the capacity for recalling.

"I was twenty years old. In my mind, I was on the way to stardom. To the studio, I was just another starlet who, if she is lucky, gets small walk-on speaking parts you wouldn't notice if you weren't a very careful observer. In other words, it's unusual for a starlet to become a star. This I found out the hard way.

"For the first six months, I worked very hard. I attended classes in acting, pantomime, singing, and dancing. When I found a deserted soundstage, I would recite lines I remembered from scripts to the bare walls. I felt very comfortable alone. I would take home scripts and study them all night. I went to all the studio screenings to watch what the other actresses were doing, and why one scene was exciting and another one not. I wanted to know all I could about motion pictures.

"But the publicity people had me posing for endless still pictures. I rode in pageants wearing a costume with other starlets on the color floats, smiling, waving, and signing autographs. I did everything the studio asked me to, yet I hadn't appeared in a motion picture.

"Shortly after the studio gave me the name Marilyn Monroe, I rode on one of those floats

1947: A new starlet at Twentieth Century-Fox poses with the usual cheesecake realism.

1945: Nineteen-year-old model Norma Jeane becomes the Los Angeles version of a farm girl.

in a parade in Burbank. When someone asked me for my autograph, I had to ask, 'How do you spell Marilyn Monroe?'

"To this day, I wonder what that person must have thought."

She was quiet again. Perhaps the spelling incident expressed her feeling of distance from that artificial creation called Marilyn Monroe. The strong emotion of the earlier part of the day seemed to disappear along with an unknown twenty-year-old model and starlet named Norma Jeane.

When she continued the chronology of the newborn Marilyn, it was less the scenes that stood out than the summary:

> "Listen, Hollywood can be a cruel place. Some of those men that take advantage of a starving and lonely girl trying to make the grade as an actress should be shot."
>
> ———
>
> "Someone said to me, 'If fifty percent of the experts in Hollywood said you had no talent and should give up, what would you do?' My answer was then and still is, 'If a hundred percent told me that, all one hundred percent would be wrong.' "
>
> ———
>
> "For me, self-respect is one's greatest treasure. What does it all add up to if you don't have that? If there was only one thing in my life I was to be proud of, it's that I've never been a kept woman."
>
> ———
>
> "Personally, I think the best performance I ever gave was in *The Asphalt Jungle*. . . . The worst part I had to play was *Let's Make Love*. I didn't even have a part. . . . It was part of an old contract; I had nothing to say."

Today, even her two famous and unhappy marriages were used only to show how cheerful she was, how ready to work. Of Joe DiMaggio she said briefly, "He started complaining about my working all the time—but we're still the best of friends." Arthur Miller was discussed in the context of his script for *The Misfits*, and her opinion that its director John Huston had interfered with Miller's story. "Mr. Miller, at his best, is a great writer," she said, referring to her husband of more than four years as if to a stranger. "He's a brilliant man and a wonderful writer, but I think he is a better writer than a husband. . . . Any good script, I would do."

She summoned up memories of her career as Monroe that had mostly to do with strength and defiance; examples from the past that she seemed to need in her current crisis.

"I did everything they asked me to," she insisted, when her narrative had caught up to her recent traumatic firing from *Something's Got to Give*, just a week after her thirty-sixth birthday.

"When the director said the swimming-pool scene in the picture would look more realistic if I did the scene in the nude," she explained, "I agreed—because I was told it would make the picture more of a success artistically and commercially. I worked very hard. . . . I wanted it to be a great picture, believe me.

"Then I got sick and, well, you know the rest of the story. The newspapers and magazines have been full of what happened. And now I'm waiting. . . ." And indeed she was literally waiting in this semi-furnished house that she now called "a fortress where I can feel safe from the world." After some talk of hiring Lee Remick because she fit Marilyn's costumes, Twentieth Century-Fox had closed down the set of the unfinished film. Still, Marilyn was hoping that this studio, where Marilyn Monroe had been created all those years ago, would relent and call her back again.

"Everything they've been saying in the press is untrue," she said, still trying to counter the industry rumors that she finally had become unemployable. "I hope we can continue. . . . It can be a great picture—I know it can and so does everyone else. But all I can do is wait until they let me know."

As the interview gradually drew to a close, she proudly described the Mexican furniture she had selected to fill this barren eight-room house. Even that small story led back to the ghost of Norma Jeane: while in Mexico buying furnishings for her home, Marilyn had visited an orphanage and written a check for a one-thousand-dollar contribution, then had torn it up and written another for ten thousand dollars. That night, she had slept without sleeping pills for one of the few times in her adult life.

Only with one of Barris's last questions did the emotion of her childhood memories return. "The thing I want more than anything else?" she repeated. "I want to have children. I used to feel for every child I had, I would adopt another," she added, as if hoping to help a child like the one who still lived inside her.

"But I don't think a single person should adopt children. There's no Ma or Pa there," she said sadly, "and I know what that can be like.

"I hate living alone," she added, sounding herself like that child again, "but I'm doing it.

"I'd like to be a fine actress," she said finally, returning to defiance and pride. "Acting is my life. As far as I'm concerned, the happiest time is now. There's a future and I can't wait to get to it."

George Barris left this small white house, where Marilyn now stayed secluded except for visits to her psychiatrist and a few friends—and for a few sporadic forays to try and salvage

---

Facing page: Now a starlet, Marilyn models the Latest Hairstyles of 1947 for Twentieth Century-Fox publicity.

her career. Her outings on photographic sessions for their book project had been one of the few major commitments of the last weeks, and he sensed that his trips to her home were visits to a strange place that had become isolated from the world.

In that small, one-person house she was so proud of, the first home she had ever owned, Marilyn had insisted on showing Barris through each room—except one. "I'm sorry I can't show you my bedroom," she said of that place where she had suffered so many nights of painful insomnia or drug-induced sleep, "but it's a mess."

That was the room where police found her a few weeks later: face down on the bed, her body bare under a rumpled sheet, her hand clutching the phone as if reaching out to some invisible friend.

It was there that they photographed her for the last time.

A world-famous actress was dead. So was an unknown young girl.

Norma Jeane Baker, the real Marilyn Monroe, was born on June 1, 1926, to a Gladys Baker Mortensen, a beautiful, delicate twenty-four-year-old who was divorced from a first husband, separated from a second, and making a tenuous living from a job in a film lab that was part of Hollywood's hidden working-class world.

To Gladys, this daughter was already a symbol of hardship and rejection. She could not keep both her job and the baby, so she boarded the infant Norma Jeane for five dollars a week with a hardworking, religious family who lived across the street from Gladys's mother. Norma Jeane's real father, C. Stanley Gifford, was a salesman at the film lab. He had left Gladys on Christmas Eve after she told him a baby was on the way. He had offered her money and the advice that she was lucky to be married to Ed Mortensen. The baby would have a name. But Gladys loved this dashing, Clark Gable–looking salesman whom she had hoped would marry her after her divorce. She proudly refused his money, and was heartbroken by his advice. Though Marilyn would later tell Barris and other interviewers that her father had been killed in an accident after her birth, that was apparently the fate of Mortensen, and it was the story Gladys originally told her. Only years later did Marilyn learn that her real father had been Stanley Gifford, and that his was the face in the photograph on her mother's wall. Norma Jeane had fantasized about the handsome man in that photograph since Gladys first identified him as her father one day when five-year-old Norma Jeane had come to visit. When she was older and learned about both her illegitimacy and the name of her real father, she tried to track him down twice. When she called as Norma Jeane, Gifford simply hung up on her. When she called as Marilyn, Gifford sent his new wife to the phone

As both model and starlet, Marilyn rarely posed in anything but a bathing suit.

with the name of his lawyer in case Marilyn had "some complaint." Famous or not, his daughter was nothing to him. Neither she nor Gladys was ever to see this object of their fantasies again.

Gifford's desertion wasn't the first crushing loss Gladys had suffered. After marrying Jack Baker in Mexico when she was fifteen, and having two children by him, she had come home early from work one day to discover her husband in bed with another woman. The week she was legally separated from Baker, he kidnapped their two children. "My mother spent all of her savings trying to get her children back," Marilyn later wrote. "Finally, she traced them to Kentucky and hitchhiked to where they were . . . living in a fine house. Their father was married again and well off. She met with him but didn't ask him for anything, not even to kiss the children she had been hunting for so long. . . . Like the mother in the movie *Stella Dallas*, she went away and left them to enjoy a happier life than she could give them."

Gladys listed her first two children as dead when she entered the hospital for her third and last childbirth. Her medical bills were paid by coworkers who cared about her tragedy enough to take up a collection at the lab. Clearly, her prideful refusal of money from Gifford hadn't come from having enough money of her own. Her rejection by Gifford had already sent her into profound depression. The birth of a baby she couldn't afford combined with the loss of her first two children must certainly have deepened her despair. Depression was something she would alternately fear and succumb to for the rest of her life.

Now that parental kidnappings, women without custody, impoverished single mothers, and illegitimacy are problems that can be admitted and understood, we can only guess how much their penalty was increased by silence, isolation, and blame. Indeed, the blame goes on. Norman Mailer, Monroe's most famous biographer, condemns Gladys for listing her first two children as dead, thus proving, "it was clear she was not sentimental about babies." Even Fred Guiles, a more sympathetic writer and the biographer who has put the most effort into documenting Marilyn Monroe's childhood, hypothesizes on no evidence that Gladys might have reversed her story of infidelity, that *she* might have been discovered with a lover, thus giving her husband an "excuse to 'kidnap' his children and keep them."

In fact, even if one accepts the sexual double standard by which a wife's infidelity becomes an excuse to deprive her of her children, there are no facts to support that theory. Guiles himself notes that Gladys's colleagues and friends did not consider her to be "promiscuous" but to be a woman of good moral character. By her own testimony to Norma Jeane, Gladys had done her desperate best to regain her two children. By other people's testimony, she also did her fragile best to keep the custody of and maintain her third child. She made weekly payments to the Bolender family, who boarded Norma Jeane; she went to see her regularly on weekends, bought material for the little dresses that Ida Bolender made on her sewing machine, and took Norma Jeane to visit her furnished room in Hollywood, or to visit the lab where she worked. When Norma Jeane was only five or six, Gladys paid extra to give her daughter piano lessons. When she had whooping cough, Gladys deserted her job for days to nurse her daughter around the clock. In spite of the Bolenders' interest in adopting Norma Jeane and taking over her responsibility completely, Gladys steadfastly refused to take this easier way out.

It was while visiting her mother's furnished room that Norma Jeane noticed the one and only picture on the wall—a handsome dark-haired man with a mustache and a slouch hat—and was told, "That's your father."

"I felt so excited, I almost fell off the chair," Marilyn wrote in her autobiography. "It felt so good to have a father, to be able to look at his picture and know I belonged to him. . . . That was my first happy time. . . ." From then on, she conjured up fantasies that she would replay in her mind over and over again. When Norma Jeane walked home from school in the rain, she imagined her father waiting at home and worrying that she had not worn her rubbers—though in fact she owned no rubbers. Lying in the hospital with complications after having her tonsils out, his abandoned daughter imagined this handsome man entering the ward "while the other patients looked on with disbelief and envy . . . and I gave him dialogue, too. 'You'll be well in a few days, Norma Jeane. I'm very proud of the way you're behaving, not crying all the time like other girls.' "

But her fantasies had no more power to rescue than the photograph. As Marilyn remembered, "I could never get him in my largest, deepest daydream to take off his hat and sit down."

Gladys had a dream about her daughter, too. "One day my mother came to call," Marilyn wrote of a time when she was still with the Bolenders. "I was in the kitchen washing dishes. She stood looking at me without talking. When I turned around, I saw there were tears in her eyes, and I was surprised. 'I'm going to build a house for you and me to live in,' she said. 'It's going to be painted white and have a backyard.' And she went away."

By borrowing money, working double shifts at the lab, furnishing sparsely and on the installment plan, and renting most of it to an English couple who were playing minor parts in movies, Gladys actually managed that house. It was a small white bungalow, and even had a secondhand white piano for Norma Jeane to play. She finally moved there when she was six.

Suddenly, Norma Jeane discovered a very different world from that of the churchgoing, puritanical Bolenders. They had loved her, but they also ran a very strict household in which she did chores, was chastised with a razor strop, attended church twice a week, and learned to sing only such acceptable songs as "Jesus Loves Me." She was also conscientiously reminded that the Bolenders were not her real parents whenever she hopefully referred to them as Ma and Pa. In the new white bungalow, she lived with her real mother for the first time. The fun-loving English couple taught her to juggle and dance, to sing many popular songs, and to speak without the working-class "ain'ts" and "it don'ts" of her early years. The white piano had the added glamour of having once belonged to Fredric March. This shy little girl was encouraged to talk, to sing, and to emerge from her quiet shell.

Most magically of all, Norma Jeane discovered the movies. Grauman's Egyptian Theatre was nearby, and children were admitted to this exotic palace for only a dime. It was a cheap baby-sitter that eased the busy schedules of Gladys and the English couple. Soon the movies were Norma Jeane's passion: a daydreaming refuge from her past, from the shy inferiority she still felt with other children at school, and from her mother's occasional moodiness.

The next year was a more carefree time than Norma Jeane had ever known. She discovered Clark Gable and Jean Harlow, Fred Astaire and Ginger Rogers, Claudette Colbert, Joan Crawford, and all the shimmering giants of the fantastic screen. She especially loved musicals, and would sit through them over and over again, sometimes missing dinner. Aside from Clark Gable, who reminded her of her father's photograph (and who she sometimes told other children *was* her father), she loved the blonde and glamorous Jean Harlow. Years later, Anita Loos, who wrote scripts for Harlow and had met Monroe, saw so much of Harlow in Marilyn's screen presence that she felt it could not have been an accident.

The little white bungalow with white furniture and the white piano came to symbolize a new freedom and happiness to Norma Jeane. White would remain her favorite color—used for houses, rooms, and costumes in her most important films—for the rest of her life.

But this idyll was brief. Working double shifts to pay the bills, keeping up the household and a cheerful face for her daughter had put an extra strain on Gladys. She could feel the depressions she feared so much coming back. In fact, she had rented the whole house to the English couple, with only two rooms reserved for herself and Norma Jeane, so that her daughter would have a home even if those depressions kept Gladys from functioning. As her private terrors increased, she tried to conceal them by working the night shift and staying away from home even on weekends.

One rainy morning in January 1934, Gladys called the lab to say she was not able to work. She finally had become immobilized in her own interior world. On the advice of Gladys's friend and coworker, Grace McKee—the Aunt Grace who soon would become Norma Jeane's legal guardian—the English couple called an ambulance to rescue Gladys from the staircase where she had hidden herself, hysterical and inconsolable. Attendants forcibly removed her and strapped her to a stretcher. She was taken first to the nearby hospital where her daughter had been born, then to the same mental hospital where her own mother, the beautiful Della Monroe, had died of a manic seizure barely two years after Norma Jeane's birth. Except for brief periods, Gladys would not emerge from an institution for the rest of her daughter's life.

The seven-year-old Norma Jeane came home from school to find her mother "gone to hospital for a while," as the English couple gently put it. The little girl seemed almost resigned, as if she had known this time of freedom could not last. As Gladys had requested,

the couple kept her with them. They sold some of the furniture to help maintain mortgage payments as long as they could; then moved to furnished rooms when they finally had to let the expensive house go. Grace McKee also helped pay Norma Jeane's expenses, a generous gesture toward a little girl who was only the daughter of a friend, but a year later, the makeshift arrangement came to a halt. The English couple could not find enough work in movies, and had to return home.

According to the detailed research by Guiles in *Legend: The Life and Death of Marilyn Monroe*, Norma Jeane's path to the orphanage wasn't as direct as her own foreshortened memory of it. In addition to that year with the English couple, there were a few more months with another family found by Grace McKee. They were drawn to this quiet, uncertain, love-hungry eight-year-old who was close to their own daughter's age, and wanted to adopt her before moving to New Orleans. There was also a former coworker of Gladys's at the lab who was willing to adopt Norma Jeane and keep her in California where she could visit her mother. But the idea of legally giving up her third and last child, the only family she had left, only increased Gladys's depression. From the hospital, she refused the legal permission necessary for either adoption. She could neither take care of Norma Jeane nor bear to let her go.

On September 13, 1935, Grace, who was now Norma Jeane's legal guardian, took the nine-year-old girl on that terrifying, long-remembered trip to the orphanage. To a grown-up, it may have seemed a sad but only temporary solution. To a little girl, it loomed as the indefinite, doom-struck future. After six years of having to be reminded by the Bolenders that her real mother was the red-haired lady she saw on weekends, and then learning from that lady that her father was only a photograph, after less than a year of living with her mother, followed by nearly two years with two other temporary "families," her tenuous sense of belonging anywhere collapsed.

In later years, when the famous Marilyn Monroe talked about her painful childhood, the Bolenders would protest that she had been well cared for, that they had treated her as they did their own adopted son who was close to her own age. The orphanage where she felt so deprived and abandoned would point out that children there were regarded as members of a big family, with no more regimentation or deprivation than any other family that size. Many of Marilyn Monroe's biographers would accuse her of lying about her childhood suffering because she sometimes exaggerated facts: for instance, that she had been in "a dozen" foster homes, when the reality was a half dozen; or that her mother's nervous breakdown had occurred when she was only five, as she had told Barris, instead of the reality, seven; or that she had hidden Gladys's life in a mental institution by telling reporters for the first few years of her Hollywood starlet days that her mother was dead. Even Jim Dougherty, who had reason to know and believe Norma Jeane's family abandonment, objected in his book, *The Secret Happiness of Marilyn Monroe*, to the idea that Norma Jeane had been deprived. The Dougherty family had lived in a tent during the Depression, and his wife's childhood in foster homes seemed to him better fed and better housed than his own had been.

But of all Marilyn's stories of her early years, the account of rape by an elderly boarder when she was eight was most disbelieved. Guiles, the careful researcher, discounted the story because he could not find one of Norma Jeane's foster families who also ran a boardinghouse. On the other hand, he did support through interviews the fact that Aunt Grace's husband, Doc Goddard, once stumbled drunk into the teenage Norma Jeane's bedroom, and terrified her by sitting on the bed and giving her what Guiles described as a "French kiss." Though that episode took place several years later than Marilyn's account of a rape, Guiles allows that she might have disguised her attacker if he was indeed married to the woman who was her legal guardian. Neither he nor other biographers pursued the possibility of the Englishman, though he and his wife could have been considered boarders in the white bungalow, and Norma Jeane was then an eight-year-old. In many cases, the tendency to disbelieve Marilyn's story is reinforced by Jim Dougherty's remembrance of his sixteen-year-old bride as a technical virgin, and thus someone who could not have been raped. Norman Mailer flatly asserts that her virginity as a bride makes the story of her childhood rape impossible. He seems unaware of the statistics that show many rapes, especially those of very young children, consist of oral and other sexual humiliations, not intercourse. Dougherty and Mailer especially seem to depend only on their own imaginations of what a rape should be.

In any case, childhood memories are prisms, not panes of glass. Details may loom large in the eyes of our smaller selves, while important events lie beyond our vision or understanding. Most of what Marilyn told Barris and other reporters differs in detail but is consistent in emotion. What impressed friends and lovers who actually listened to her—as opposed to biographers like Mailer and Guiles who never met her—was her emotional honesty. Facts may have been forgotten, or exaggerated to account for strong feelings, but Marilyn remained true to her memories of Norma Jeane's emotional experience. From Arthur Miller and from friends, there comes a sense that, even when she tried to pretend an emotion—for instance, to be confident or gay when she did not feel it—some underlying honesty still gave her away. Whatever its facts, her memory of being sexually humiliated as a child, and then of being humiliated again by disbelief, seemed too full of pain to be artificial. Certainly, the stammering she attributed to that trauma was real.

One of her tragedies may have been growing up in a time when Freudian theory had convinced many people (perhaps Marilyn's own later psychiatrists) that female children wanted and so fantasized rape by fathers or father figures. It was also a time when the Depression had focused American attention more on the physical suffering of children who lacked food and shelter than on the damage caused by emotional neglect. As a result, children's sexual testimony largely was disbelieved, and sincere efforts to help children were focused on providing nutrition, safety, and shelter.

During World War II, a few years after Norma Jeane's time in an orphanage, thousands of children were evacuated from the air raids and poor rations of London during the Blitz, and placed with volunteer families or group homes in the English countryside or even in other countries. It was only postwar studies comparing these children to others left behind that

Marilyn with Joe DiMaggio who insisted she wear such modest clothes in private.

opened the eyes of many experts to the damage caused by emotional neglect. In spite of living in bombed-out ruins and constant fear of attack, the children who had been left with their mothers and families tended to fare better than those who had been evacuated to physical safety. Emotional security, continuity, a sense of being loved unconditionally for oneself—all those turn out to be as important to a child's development as all but the most basic food and shelter.

It was exactly these emotional basics that Norma Jeane lacked. And she was deprived of them in the earliest years of her life, when the resulting damage to a sense of self is most difficult to repair.

Once she found her first brief but never-forgotten taste of unconditional love with her beloved Aunt Ana, Marilyn's memory seems to have exaggerated the time that it lasted, as if this rare and bright light in her life had made the shadows around it disappear.

In fact, she was not taken directly to Aunt Ana's house from the orphanage, as she told Barris. In late June 1937, when Aunt Grace made good on her promise of rescue, she took the eleven-year-old Norma Jeane to live with a husband and wife in Compton who ran a small business out of their home. Grace had married Doc Goddard, a divorced man ten years younger than she was, while Norma Jeane was in the orphanage. His three children were living with them, and Grace did not feel she could also take in Norma Jeane.

For a long summer, Norma Jeane helped her new "mother" in Compton load and deliver cartons to small stores throughout Los Angeles County. When she complained to her Aunt Grace that she was spending all her time riding in her new family's battered car, Aunt Grace found her another home with a couple who made their meager living by keeping several other "county children." There, an alcoholic husband presented another problem of instability. Grace was finally forced to take Norma Jeane into her own home, and into the bedroom of her stepdaughter, who was two years younger than Norma Jeane. She entered junior high a term behind her classmates. The irregularity of Norma Jeane's life had caused her to fall back in school. In the seventh grade, but already tall and well developed, she became even more self-conscious.

But Norma Jeane was befriended by an aunt of Grace McKee Goddard's. Her name was Ana Lower. Though she lived some distance away, Norma Jeane began spending every Sunday with this woman in her early sixties, accompanying her to Christian Science services, and eagerly drinking in her philosophy and affection. Though Ana Lower had never married or had children, she instinctively seemed to understand the support Norma Jeane needed, and to nurture the child inside this teenager who looked so deceptively mature.

In fact, Norma Jeane was a young girl who might not betray her presence in a room by so much as a cough, and so was called "Mouse" by the Goddards; yet in junior high school she found herself the object of fervent male attention. For all her "precocious curves," as Marilyn later wrote, "I was as unsensual as a fossil. But I seemed to affect people quite otherwise." Norma Jeane's refuge was Aunt Ana's house or the movies. At the Goddards', she would close herself into her bedroom alone, and act out all the parts in any movie she had just seen. With the encouragement first of the orphanage matron, then of Aunt Grace, she also had begun experimenting with makeup that reminded her of the movies, but increased her oddly grown-up looks.

It was into this same bedroom that the drunken six-foot-two-inch Doc Goddard barged one evening, bestowing the "French kiss" for which Guiles reported he was sorry when sober. But this treatment from a man Norma Jeane had regarded as a substitute father and called Daddy was shocking enough to confide in Aunt Ana. Whatever the discussion with Grace and her husband, Aunt Ana then decided to take the fourteen-year-old into her own home.

Norma Jeane spent only a little more than a year living with Aunt Ana in the top half of a modest two-family house, but she had a loving, focused presence in her life for the first time. She was still a county child with public-support checks paying for her keep, her legal guardian was still Aunt Grace, and her own mother was still in a mental hospital, but Norma Jeane would remember this time as one of the happiest, and Aunt Ana as her most important influence, for the rest of her life.

This happy period was cut short when Doc Goddard was about to move his family to West Virginia, and Aunt Grace began to look for an alternative for Norma Jeane. Whether Grace's motive was keeping her ten-years-younger husband from straying, protecting Norma Jeane, honoring her friend Gladys's desire to have her daughter nearby, or all three, she never proposed taking the fifteen-year-old Norma Jeane with them. Whether Aunt Ana was persuaded by Grace's arguments that Norma Jeane needed the protection of marriage, or by her own feeling of being too old to take over the responsibility of legal guardianship for a teenager, she didn't stop Grace's new plan. In later life, Marilyn never blamed Aunt Ana for arranging her teenage marriage—but she did blame Aunt Grace.

After suggesting the marriage to the Dougherty family, with whom the twenty-year-old Jim was still living—and after a few dates between Jim and Norma Jeane—Aunt Grace instructed the teenager to explain her illegitimacy to Jim in case this still shameful status was a bar to the marriage. It was not; but later, Marilyn said this was the first time she had been sure that her father and mother were not married, or known that the name Mortensen on her own birth certificate belonged to her mother's second husband.

Before leaving for West Virginia, Aunt Grace arranged to have the wedding performed in the home of friends. The winding staircase in their front hall would make the ceremony "just like in the movies," she assured Norma Jeane. With both this guardian and her mother absent, and no known father in sight, it was Ana Lower who gave her "niece" away. Marilyn had exaggerated when she recalled "six mothers weeping" at her wedding, but the Bolenders did come for the occasion. It was the last time Norma Jeane would ever see them. The marriage ceremony was conducted by a minister of the Christian Church who had taught Jim to hunt and shoot when he was a boy.

Having been born "Mortensen," and gone to school as "Baker," she was now "Norma Jeane Dougherty." Later she would revert on occasion to "Baker," the name of her mother's

Marilyn with husband-to-be Arthur Miller in 1956.

first husband; and she also used "Jean Norman," at the suggestion of her modeling agency. Later still, as a starlet, she would choose "Monroe" for its alliteration with the studio-chosen first name of "Marilyn." Ironically, she became famous with the family name of both her maternal grandmother and her mother, whose shared fate of desertion by men and depression would be continued to the third generation.

In early 1946, Gladys called Grace Goddard, who had returned with her husband to California, to say that she would like to try living outside an institution again. It was decided that mother and daughter could live together in the downstairs apartment of Ana Lower's house—Jim Dougherty was away at sea. The nineteen-year-old Norma Jeane was making her living as a model in the absence of her husband, and trying to become a starlet.

They slept in the same bed, and Gladys tried to make herself useful to her daughter by looking after the small apartment, answering the phone, and taking messages of modeling assignments and studio casting calls. Once, she even got painstakingly dressed in a white dress, white shoes, and a new picture hat to make a surprise call on Emmeline Snively, whose modeling agency she believed had rescued her daughter. After fervently discussing Norma Jeane's career with the astonished Miss Snively, Gladys shook her hand and said, "I only came so I could thank you personally for what you've been doing for Norma Jeane. You've given her a whole new life."

But that was probably one of Gladys's few outings on her own. It was hard for the long-institutionalized Gladys to be alone. Norma Jeane was gone from the apartment most of the day. When she decided to move out of the apartment and into the Studio Club, a rooming house for starlets, Gladys's only company was the elderly Aunt Ana who lived upstairs. Gradually, she even stopped going upstairs.

And it must have been hard for Norma Jeane, too. There was the pressure on her starlet's small salary of helping to support her mother, and the occasional shopping sprees that Gladys's mood swings produced. Before her mother's arrival her small earnings had barely paid for her own food and professional expenses, and Dougherty had angrily cut off her allotment as soon as she wrote him about a divorce. There were also fearful memories. "I kept hearing the terrible noise on the stairs and my mother screaming and laughing as they led her out of the home she had tried to build for me," Marilyn later said. Each time she came home to that apartment, she must have worried about what she would find.

However, when Norma Jeane moved into the Studio Club, Gladys seemed to accept this as necessary to her daughter's career. Dougherty had met his mother-in-law for the first time earlier that year when he was on leave. In August he saw her again when he met Norma Jeane at the apartment instead of the Studio Club to discuss signing the divorce papers. If the dissolution of this marriage had not been already inevitable on personal grounds, Gladys seemed to approve it as a work necessity. Miss Snively had made clear that movie studios did not want to hire a starlet who was married and might waste their investment by getting pregnant.

Norma Jeane sometimes stopped by to see her mother between studio appointments, and was alarmed that Gladys was withdrawing more and more into one of her refuges: an obsession with religion.

After just seven months of living outside an institution, Gladys asked the hospital to take her back. Norma Jeane was relieved. She was free now to begin a new life. This ghost from her childhood, a ghost whose fate she feared she would share, has outlived her by many years. First Marilyn, and then money left in Marilyn's will, have supported Gladys in and out of institutions; she was never to live an independent life again.

In her notes for an autobiography, Marilyn recalled being told to say "Mama" to "a pretty woman who never smiled" and who visited her at the Bolenders'. "I'd seen her often before, but I hadn't quite known who she was.

"When I said, 'Hello mama,' this time, she stared at me. She had never kissed me or held me in her arms or hardly spoken to me. I didn't know anything about her then, but a few years later I learned a number of things.

"When I think of her now, my heart hurts twice as much as it used to when I was a little girl. It hurts me for both of us."

In 1963, the year after Marilyn Monroe's death, Dr. W. Hugh Missildine, a psychiatrist, published a book called *Your Inner Child of the Past*. It was an analysis of adult emotional problems based on his nine years as director of the Children's Mental Health Center in Columbus, Ohio. Without the artificial language or gender-based theories of Freud, he simply wrote what he had concluded from observation.

He believed that the child we used to be lives on inside us. It is difficult for us to change that child's patterns because they feel like "home." Recognizing this compelling self of the past can help to keep us from repeating history. Otherwise, we may continue to treat ourselves—and others—as that child was once treated. At worst, such repetition is destructive. Even at best, we are following a pattern we did not choose for ourselves.

In identifying common excesses experienced by children, and so reported by them as adults, he used postwar studies on the damage caused by emotional neglect—damage that can occur even among the well-to-do without physical neglect. One chapter outlined the characteristics of an adult who is still controlled by the neglected child inside. Here is Missildine's "Index of Suspicion" for such an adult. He could almost be speaking about and to Marilyn:

> If you have difficulty in feeling close to others and in "belonging" to a group, drift in and out of relationships casually because people do not seem to mean much to you, if you feel you lack an identity of your own, suffer intensely from anxiety and loneliness and yet keep people at a distance, you should suspect neglect as the troublemaking pathogenic factor in your childhood. An additional clue suggesting neglect: prolonged separation from your parents, particularly your mother, by death, divorce, hospitalization or because of parental activities and interests.

Missildine described other common characteristics of such women, as well as men, though using the generic "he" of the day:

> The childhood of persons who suffered from neglect usually reveals a father who somehow wasn't a father and a mother who somehow wasn't a mother. Thus, in adult life, the neglected "child of the past" maintains the security of this familiar emptiness. . . . The relationships of persons who suffered from neglect in childhood resemble those of an actor to his audience. In childhood such a person may have discovered that he could win . . . momentary attention and love, through his achievements. . . . In such circumstances a child learns to expect nothing but applause. More than momentary warmth and love do not exist. . . . Closeness threatens the security of neglect on which his "child of the past" has been nourished. To such a person, closeness is frightening, binding and entrapping. . . .
>
> Superficially, the famous movie star with her numerous conquests and marriages, the world statesman and his lonely, melancholy wisdom, and the woman whose life consists of serving others do not seem to have been particularly neglected. . . . Yet often they are deeply unhappy in their continuing self-neglect. . . .
>
> . . . It is not at all unusual for the individual who has suffered the loss of a parent for any reason . . . to create in his childhood fantasies a highly idealized parent. In his imagination this idealized and loving parent would correct all the difficulties he encounters, would appreciate his efforts, indulge him endlessly. . . .

A back view of the small, Mexican-style house in Brentwood where Marilyn died. She was especially proud of having her own swimming pool.

This bedroom was the one room of her house Barris didn't see, and the room where she died on the night of August 4, 1962.

However, if continued into adolescence and adult life, the idealized fantasy parent may prevent formation of close relationships with members of the opposite sex. . . . A girl who has lost her father may idealize him and reject men who might make excellent marriage partners because she feels they are lacking in the finer qualities of a gentleman and a scholar.

. . . Most individuals who suffered from neglect in childhood . . . actively seek social participation, sexual love and affection—"can't get enough of it," as one such girl declared. Once they have overcome an initial timidity, they may plunge into any relationship that seems to promise companionship, affection, closeness or excitement.

The lack of mothering in childhood tends to dominate the sexual activities. . . . Such a person is interested in and wants tender, mothering love—not sexuality—and tends to convert the partner into a mothering figure. . . .

The inability of the person who has suffered from neglect in childhood to contribute much emotionally to a relationship often causes its disintegration. Its maintenance is left to the other partner—and he tends to move off because he is tired of the burden. . . .

Earlier in the work, Missildine noted:

Often the person whose childhood has been scarred by neglect becomes expert in exploiting others. . . . He knows just how to stimulate interest and sympathy in himself. And he will demand love and affection, constant attention and emotional support. . . . But this is a one-way street. . . .

. . . Many such people, particularly women, are drawn into theatrical and movie work because, in this work and atmosphere, they can create a fantasy identity. Their inner feelings about themselves are so despairing that they do not feel they can pay attention to these feelings. As one such woman once put it: "When you're a nobody, the only way to be somebody is to be somebody else."

As you read and think about Marilyn, remember Norma Jeane.

WORK AND MONEY, SEX AND POLITICS

I am not interested in money. I just want to be wonderful.

—*Marilyn Monroe*

That famous dictum of Marilyn's was quoted to Pete Martin, a journalist writing a book about her in the 1950s, by a man in the legal department of Twentieth Century-Fox. In advising her on a new contract she was bargaining for, he had suggested that she sign it in the existing tax year rather than waiting until the following one, thus saving herself money—and she refused.

Marilyn was obsessed with her career, with becoming a good actress as well as a famous movie star, but she cared very little about money and possessions. She wanted not power but love. Indeed, she sometimes acted against her own financial self-interest, and showed concern for business by forming her own production company only when she feared she was being exploited by Hollywood. To the end, her life-style and habits were fairly simple.

That she often ignored her own security was more than just the neglected Norma Jeane re-creating a feeling of "home" by treating herself as she had been treated. It was also part of her emotional connection to ordinary people like those of her childhood—working-class families who were struggling through the Depression, people for whom poverty was no shame and the chance to work hard was a gift.

Even as a penniless starlet, invited as decoration to Hollywood parties where men risked thousands on a casual card game, she didn't want to become one of the rich. "When I saw them hand hundred- and even thousand-dollar bills to each other," she wrote, "I felt something bitter in my heart. I remembered how much twenty-five cents and even nickels meant to the people I had known, how happy ten dollars would have made them, how a hundred dollars would have changed their whole lives. I remembered my Aunt Grace and me waiting in line at the Holmes Bakery to buy a sackful of bread. . . . And I remembered how she had gone with one of her lenses missing from her glasses for three months because she couldn't afford the fifty cents to buy its replacement. I remembered all the sounds and smells of poverty, the fright in people's eyes when they lost jobs, and the way they skimped and drudged in order to get through the week."

From those people, Norma Jeane had learned to work hard. Habits gained while doing chores in the orphanage and foster homes or watching the job struggles of her mother and her Aunt Grace were reinforced by her own need for approval. They helped her keep an immaculate apartment as a teenage bride and win an E for excellence when she worked spraying fuselages at a defense plant. She was also remembered by photographers as the rare model who asked for criticism and wanted to learn every aspect of composing a good photograph.

From them, she also learned the importance of dreams in lives whose realities were hard. As Norma Jeane, imagination and fantasy had been her only refuge. "I loved playing pretend games," Marilyn said of her fascination with acting, "and I led all the other children into making up play games, and taking different parts. And I'd listen to 'The Lone Ranger' and get terribly excited. Not at the horses and the chases and the guns but . . . the *drama*. The wondering of how it would be for each person in that situation. . . . There are techniques to be learned, and it's hard work. But it still seems sort of like play to me, and something you want terribly to do."

When she herself became rich, it couldn't change the lives of ordinary people, and only made her feel estranged from them. It couldn't even change her own sense of being an outsider among the well-to-do, where her lack of education and social skills made her feel personally out of place. But, as an actress, she could offer everyday moviegoers the hope and dreams that had built a fantasy escape for Norma Jeane. "Even if all I had to do in a scene was just to come in and say 'Hi,' " Marilyn explained of her obsession with work, "I've always felt that the people ought to get their money's worth, and that this is an obligation of mine, to give them the best you can get from me." Response from working people seemed to mean as much to Marilyn as praise from movie critics, or coveted invitations to the same Beverly Hills parties she once had decorated as an interchangeable starlet. When street crowds yelled their approval at premieres, she seemed to forget her terror of appearing in public. When truck drivers called a friendly greeting in the street, or children asked for her autograph, or old people stopped to say she made them proud, she was delighted and touched. She considered herself one of them—and they seemed to sense that. Indeed, this populist support was one of the few things that could buoy up her shaky self-confidence. In Korea, where she went to entertain the troops, she was honestly amazed and moved to find an audience of thirteen thousand G.I.'s waiting in the freezing cold. When the crowd called for her over and over again, she insisted on braving the chill in a strapless dress and open sandals so she wouldn't disappoint them. "It was the first time," she explained later, "that I ever felt I had an effect on people."

Given her obsession with public stardom, the poverty of her early days in Hollywood, and her use of sex as a friendly reward to men whom she trusted to understand or help her, many biographers have been skeptical of her protestations that she was never "kept," or her angry and fearful response to being sexually "used." As she had told George Barris, shortly before her death, "If there's only one thing in my life I was to be proud of, it's that I've never been a kept woman." In those last months when she was out of work and had even less sense of self

than usual, she raged and wept at the idea that men might be using her "only as a plaything."

"Maybe it was the nickel Mr. Kimmel once gave me . . . ," she wrote, using a name that referred to the old man she said had sexually attacked her as an eight-year-old, "but men who tried to buy me with money made me sick. There were plenty of them. The mere fact that I turned down offers ran my price up. . . . I didn't take their money, and they couldn't get by my front door, but I kept riding in their limousines and sitting beside them in swanky places. There was always a chance a job and not another wolf might spot you."

There is not only her testimony, but the financial facts of her life to support the belief that she refused gifts of clothes and expensive apartments from the various men who wanted to "keep" her. Most of her pre-stardom days in Hollywood were spent cleaning by hand and rewearing the same two or three dresses, eating meals at drugstore counters when she had little money, and living on peanut butter and raw hamburger in her room to keep up her energy when she had even less. Her small income as a starlet-in-training went for acting lessons in her drive for self-improvement. When she got broke enough in those early model-ing and acting days, she seems to have exchanged sex for small sums of money from men she didn't have to see again. Lena Pepitone, a maid who worked for her in New York, says Marilyn told her of trading sex for fifteen dollars in pocket money from a man she met in a bar when Jim Dougherty was away at sea, and that there were a few other such incidents after that. Acting teacher Lee Strasberg also told an interviewer that Marilyn said she had worked as a call girl at conventions, and that she felt damaged by the experience. No independent evidence has come to light to support these stories: Marilyn may have been dramatizing the deprivation of her background, as she sometimes did, as if to justify her real feelings of being deprived.

And, as Patricia Newcomb, her friend and press assistant, has explained, "Marilyn Monroe never told anybody everything."

But even if the most sordid of these stories were true, they seem to parallel the famous calendar incident. After refusing other nude modeling jobs, Marilyn finally agreed to pose for the nude calendar for only fifty dollars because it was the exact sum she needed to retrieve her old car. Even though waiting until she was desperate went against her own financial self-interest, she seems to have resisted pridefully, and then given in only when she thought there was no other way out.

"In Hollywood a girl's virtue is much less important than her hairdo," she wrote bitterly. "You're judged by how you look, not by what you are. Hollywood's a place where they'll pay you a thousand dollars for a kiss, and fifty cents for your soul. I know, because I turned down the first offer often enough and held out for the fifty cents."

When she felt she did have a choice, her standards were romantic, even idealistic. Johnny Hyde, an agent thirty years her senior who helped her greatly with her early career, knew very well that Marilyn loved him only as a father and a friend, but he also knew that his heart condition left him only a short time to live. Because he loved Marilyn and wanted her to inherit his million-dollar estate, he pleaded with her to marry him. She refused. Though Hyde was one of the few people in her life whom she trusted completely, she told him that marrying for reasons other than love "wouldn't be fair."

In his biography of Marilyn, Norman Mailer admits to being mystified by her refusal to marry for money. Given the facts of her need, plus his view of her character—he calls her promiscuous and "a queen of a castrator"—Mailer treats her refusal as inexplicable. In fact, he missed the romanticism that governed her behavior and was the legacy of her Depression childhood. From families that owned little but their own good names, she had inherited the fierce pride of the poor. Because she was sometimes forced to give in, to sell herself partially, she was all the more fearful of being bought totally. "What have you got to lose?" asked a friend who was urging the marriage to Hyde. "Myself," Marilyn said. "I'm only going to marry for one reason—love."

As for her frequent use of sex, Mailer assumes that this meant hostility toward men. In fact, she seemed so hungry for the love and approval she had been denied in childhood, particularly from a father, that she submerged her own physical pleasure, and offered sex in return for male support and affection. By her own testimony to friends and from that of lovers, she never—or rarely—had orgasms, as if the child inside her needed to absorb years of affection before a sexual adult could be born. Henry Rosenfeld, a New York dress manufacturer who met her in her early twenties and remained a close friend until her death, explained that "Marilyn thought sex got you closer, made you a closer friend. She told me she hardly ever had an orgasm, but she was very unselfish. She tried above all to please the opposite sex. Ah, but it wasn't just sex. She could be so happy and gay. How I remember that laughter!"

In an interview two years before she died, Marilyn told writer Jaik Rosenstein that sex also had been part of her first work assignments. "When I started modeling, it was like part of the job," she explained. "All the girls did . . . and if you didn't go along, there were twenty-five girls who would." In Hollywood, she added, "You know that when a producer calls an actress into his office to discuss a script, that isn't all he has in mind. . . . She can go hungry and she might have to sleep in her car, but she doesn't mind that a bit—if she can only get the part. I know because I've done both, lots of times. And I've slept with producers. I'd be a liar if I said I didn't. . . ." She trusted Rosenstein not to use those off-the-record quotes, and he didn't, not until long after her death when the sexual double standard was more forgiving. Thanks to Anthony Summers, who accumulated these quotes in his book *Goddess: The Secret Lives of Marilyn Monroe*, we also know that she told W. J. Weatherby, a British journalist, "You can't sleep your way into being a star, though. It takes much, much more. But it helps. A lot of actresses get their first chance that way. Most of the men are such horrors, they deserve all they can get out of them!"

Marilyn supplied sex so that she would be allowed to work, but not so that she wouldn't have to work.

The Depression idea that a job was a coveted opportunity, a gift, not a right, was a good preparation for Hollywood. "I knew how third-rate I was," Marilyn wrote with characteristic self-deprecation. "I could actually feel my lack of talent, as if it were cheap clothes I was wearing inside. But, my God, how I wanted to learn! To change, to improve! I didn't want anything else. Not men, not money, not love, but the ability to act. With the arc lights on me and the camera pointed at me, I suddenly knew myself. How clumsy, empty, uncultured I was! A sullen orphan with a goose egg for a head.

"But I would change. . . . I spent my salary on dramatic lessons, on dancing lessons, and singing lessons. I bought books to read. I sneaked scripts off the set and sat up alone in my room reading them out loud in front of the mirror. And an odd thing happened to me. I fell in love with myself—not how I was but how I was going to be."

In fact, whether or not she was confident enough to know it, she already had an extraordinary luminescence and vulnerability that set her apart. Marion Marshall, who would later marry actor Robert Wagner, remembered meeting her as Norma Jeane when they both were applying for a job as bathing-suit models. "Marilyn was the most spectacular girl I ever met, not particularly beautiful, but she radiated a special dynamism," she explained. "I remember, when I first saw her, she arrived late as usual, after all the other girls. I'm sitting with all these very sophisticated models, dressed in silks, with the gloves and the hat and all that, and Marilyn came in a little scoop-necked gingham sundress, her hair unbleached and unstraightened. When she walked in, it was like the room stopped, and everyone in the room knew she was going to get the job, and she did."

But the Marilyn-who-was-going-to-be needed to lower her squeaky speaking voice, to train her soft but pleasant singing voice, and to learn how to drop barriers of childhood isolation so that internal emotion could come through. She also had to memorize scripts, camera instructions, and makeup procedures, and acquire the technical ability to re-create the same scene over and over again. Acting coach Natasha Lytess was enlisted to help with voice-lowering and general training. Their relationship would last seven years, during which Natasha took Marilyn into her own home, rescued her from one suicide attempt—when she was grief-stricken following Johnny Hyde's death—and came both to feel used by Marilyn and to love her. ("Don't love me," Marilyn pleaded with Natasha, "just teach me.") Marilyn herself sought out Michael Chekhov, the nephew of the playwright, who had studied under Stanislavsky and then given up his own acting career to become a teacher. With Chekhov she undertook such challenges as *The Cherry Orchard* and Cordelia in *King Lear*. Inspired by the cultured and well-read Lytess and Chekhov, Marilyn nourished her habit of hungry but random reading and tried to fathom everything from biographies of Abraham Lincoln, her childhood hero, to such abstract treatises as *The Thinking Body*, a study of the relationship between body and mind. She never stopped feeling inferior because she had not even finished high school, and she never stopped trying to make up for it.

But in movies, her growing number of bit parts were a far cry from Shakespeare. Given the background she was escaping, some had an added irony. *Dangerous Years*, released in 1947, gave her a small role as a brassy waitress in a drama of juvenile delinquency. The murderer was a boy raised in an orphanage as Norma Jeane had been. The following year, *Ladies of the Chorus* cast her with Adele Jergens as mother-and-daughter chorines, and required Marilyn, the child who obsessively longed for a father, to hold a baby doll in her arms while singing

"Every Baby Needs a Da Da Daddy." After a particularly miserable, insecure period in which her starlet's contract was allowed to lapse for a second time—first by Twentieth Century-Fox and then by Columbia Pictures—she won a small part in *Love Happy*, a Marx Brothers movie in which she unveiled her very sexy walk.

Thanks to *Love Happy* and the publicity tour she did for it, Marilyn began to get some attention from the press and public. After playing another chorine in a Dan Dailey feature, *A Ticket to Tomahawk*, agent Johnny Hyde helped her get a reading for the role of a crooked lawyer's mistress in her first grade-A movie—John Huston's *The Asphalt Jungle*—but it was Marilyn's agonizingly prepared audition that won the part. As one of the best movies of 1950, *The Asphalt Jungle* got favorable reviews that included Marilyn's small role. More important, Johnny Hyde successfully suggested to Joe Mankiewicz, writer-director of the classic *All About Eve*, that he cast her in that memorable mistress role because of it. She was now back under contract to Twentieth Century-Fox and getting fan mail the studio executives couldn't ignore.

It was on this Mankiewicz set that Marilyn, who was largely innocent of newspapers and politics, got one of her first tastes of the McCarthyite atmosphere of the 1950s. As part of her unguided self-education, she had picked up *The Autobiography of Lincoln Steffens*, a book she described in her own autobiography as "bitter but strong. . . . [He] knew all about poor people and about injustice. He knew about the lies people used to get ahead, and how smug rich people sometimes were. It was almost as if he'd lived the hard way I'd lived. I loved his book." She was surprised when Joe Mankiewicz took her aside and, as she remembered, "gave me a quiet lecture.

" 'I wouldn't go around raving about Lincoln Steffens,' he said. 'It's certain to get you into trouble. People will begin to talk of you as a radical.' "

Not understanding what a radical was, she assumed this was "a very personal attitude on Mr. Mankiewicz's part and that, genius though he was, of a sort, he was badly frightened by the Front Office or something. I couldn't imagine anybody picking on me because I admired Lincoln Steffens."

When the publicity department asked her to list the ten greatest men in the world, no doubt as a sex-story gimmick, Marilyn put Steffens's name at the top. The publicity man refused. "We'll have to omit that one," he explained patronizingly. "We don't want anybody investigating our Marilyn."

She said no more about Steffens to anyone, not even to Johnny Hyde, who was then her lover and mentor, but she continued to read the second volume secretly and kept both volumes hidden under her bed.

Two years later, Morris Carnovsky and his wife, Phoebe Brand, who had established the Actor's Lab, where Marilyn also studied, were investigated by the House Committee on Un-American Activities. Once, when Marilyn was asked about Communists, she said, "They're for the people, aren't they?" With or without knowledge, her sympathy was with the underdog.

Though Marilyn was rapidly becoming a star, she was also beginning to learn that even a star, especially an indentured contract player with little choice of scripts, could still be the underdog. She made a dozen grade-B films in rapid succession. Only three of them—*Clash by Night*, *Don't Bother to Knock*, and *Niagara*—were more than forgettable, or offered her anything other than secondary roles as a dumb blonde. One especially, *Don't Bother to Knock*, showed her as a serious actress. Anne Bancroft remembers a moment in which she was to react to Marilyn as a deranged baby-sitter who had threatened suicide. "There was just this scene of one woman seeing another woman who was helpless and in pain, and she *was* helpless and in pain," Bancroft explained. "It was so real, I responded; I really reacted to her. She moved me so that tears came into my eyes. Believe me, such moments happened rarely, if ever again, in the early things I was doing out there." Marilyn may have been playing her own experience as Norma Jeane, but that reality wasn't what interested Hollywood. In her next film, *Monkey Business*, she was back in a dumb-blonde role that gave her body all the rave reviews.

By 1952, Marilyn had graduated to stardom and the quintessential dumb blonde—Lorelei Lee in *Gentlemen Prefer Blondes*—but she loved being able to sing and dance in this movie musical like those that had been Norma Jeane's escape. The following year when that was released, so was her next film, *How to Marry a Millionaire*, a sex comedy that allowed Marilyn to wear glasses, to change her image, and to show her talent as a comedienne. Reviewers praised her gift for comedy, but one noted that sitting in the front row of a Marilyn Monroe movie was like being "smothered in baked Alaska."

After playing a wilderness version of a sexy blonde opposite Robert Mitchum in *River of No Return*, with reviews that compared her mostly to the mountainous scenery, Marilyn married Joe DiMaggio and took seven months off. After this inactivity, Marilyn welcomed a role in *There's No Business Like Show Business*. Surely this showcase of Irving Berlin songs would offer a little more class. Her own misgivings about being constantly used as a not-too-bright sex symbol were now being reinforced by her marriage to Joe DiMaggio. He was unenthusiastic about her career, and puritanical about her public use of sex. In fact, two of Marilyn's major song-and-dance numbers were ridiculed by reviewers. *The New York Times* called them "wriggling and squirming" that was "embarrassing to behold." DiMaggio was so embarrassed that according to Marilyn he agreed to pose for publicity pictures with Irving Berlin and the movie's star, Ethel Merman—but not with his own wife.

"I did what they said," Lena Pepitone remembered Marilyn saying bitterly. "And all it got me was a lot of abuse. . . . Big breasts, big ass, big deal. Can't I be anything else? . . . I was wearing this open skirt—I think they call it flamenco—with this black bra and panties underneath. The dance people kept making me flash the skirt wide open and jump around like I had a fever. . . . It was ridiculous. . . ."

Marilyn's next role, in *The Seven Year Itch*, was another sex comedy, but, under the direction of Billy Wilder, she felt it would be a classier one. Nonetheless, her typecasting as the dumb-blonde-upstairs—and especially the famous sex-icon pose of Marilyn with her white dress blowing over her head as she stands with legs apart over a subway grating—became one of the breaking points in her brief marriage to DiMaggio. In the fall of 1954, their divorce was announced and Marilyn fled Hollywood for New York. By escaping Hollywood and her Twentieth Century-Fox contract that was restricting her to scripts she didn't like, she also hoped to do more serious work by forming her own production company and studying acting. DiMaggio had wanted her to give up work—and she clearly had chosen her work.

In spite of jokes about Marilyn's acting talent, plus her own fear of performing, Strasberg was impressed with her ability as a serious dramatic actress. He took her on as a private student and ranked her with Marlon Brando as one of his most talented pupils. Even skeptical peers at Actors Studio applauded her scenes as Anna in Eugene O'Neill's *Anna Christie*; and, as Kim Stanley remembered, "It was the first time I'd ever heard applause there."

In spite of Hollywood's conviction that Marilyn wasn't smart enough to manage her own career, she astounded the film industry by negotiating as "Marilyn Monroe Productions" a new contract with Twentieth Century-Fox that vastly increased her profit and control. She then chose two films far above grade-B level: *Bus Stop*, with Joshua Logan directing this screen adaptation of a play by William Inge, and *The Prince and the Showgirl*, with Laurence Olivier as her director and costar.

In spite of her reputation for sex, not seriousness, Marilyn chose to marry the playwright Arthur Miller, whose work memorialized ordinary, working people. Some of her Hollywood advisers warned her that Miller's well-publicized troubles with the House Committee on Un-American Activities might damage her career, but she stood by him and helped to pay the legal costs of his defense.

Indeed, on the East Coast, Marilyn emerged a little from the shell of isolation created first by her childhood and then by Hollywood's artifice. She experienced more of real life in New York and Miller's Connecticut farmhouse, and even took some interest in politics in the next

few years. "Marilyn was passionate about equal rights, rights for blacks, rights for the poor," remembered one friend. "She identified strongly with the workers, and she always felt they were her people." In 1960, she became one of the sponsors of SANE, the Committee for a Sane Nuclear Policy. When an interviewer asked for her dreams or nightmares, she said, "My nightmare is the H-bomb. What's yours?" Though she still rarely read newspapers, and seemed to fear the world as a distant and mysterious place, she made an effort to be informed. When she did, her political instincts were interesting. She wrote this note to Lester Markel, then Sunday Editor of *The New York Times*:

> Lester dear,
>
> . . . About our political conversation the other day: I take it back that there isn't *anybody*. What about Rockefeller? First of all he is a Republican like the New York Times, and secondly, and most interesting, he's more liberal than many of the Democrats. Maybe he could be developed? At this time, however, Humphrey might be the only one. But who knows since it's rather hard to find out anything about him. (I have no particular paper in mind!) Of course, Stevenson might have made it if he had been able to talk to people instead of professors. Of course, there hasn't been anyone like Nixon before because the rest of them at least had souls! Ideally, Justice William Douglas would be the best President, but he has been divorced so he couldn't make it—but I've got an idea—how about Douglas for President and Kennedy for Vice-President, then the Catholics who wouldn't have voted for Douglas would vote because of Kennedy so it wouldn't matter if he *is* so divorced. Then Stevenson could be Secretary of State! . . .
>
> Love and kisses,
> Marilyn
>
> P.S. Slogans for the late '60s:
>
> "Nix on Nixon"
>
> "Over the hump with Humphrey(?)"
>
> "Stymied with Symington"
>
> "Back to Boston by Xmas—Kennedy"

In *Goddess*, Anthony Summers also reports that Marilyn called one of her press aides to ask why—only weeks after the CIA's U-2 plane had been shot down by the Soviets—a second story about an American plane trespassing Soviet airspace was treated as minor news. When the aide said perhaps this plane was not spying but doing an oceanic survey, as Washington insisted, the usually patriotic Marilyn said skeptically, "I don't know. . . . I don't trust us."

Meanwhile, in the summer of 1958, Marilyn had ended a nearly two-year hiatus in filmmaking by playing Sugar Kane in Billy Wilder's *Some Like It Hot*. Marilyn was hesitant about making a new film when she hoped to have a baby and also resisted playing a blonde so out of it that she couldn't tell Tony Curtis and Jack Lemmon in drag from real women. As she told Lena Pepitone, "I've been dumb, but not that dumb." But she took the role partly because Arthur Miller recommended it, and partly because Miller pointed out that they needed the money. It was more of a commercial success than either of the two previous films she had chosen.

In 1960, Marilyn made *Let's Make Love* with Yves Montand, a film notable mainly for the affair between its costars. Though Arthur Miller continued working on the script of *The Misfits* for his wife, the shaky marriage had essentially dissolved by the time that final film of hers was made. Marilyn's insecurity made her mistrust everyone. She had been furious at Billy Wilder for giving out public stories about her private lateness and difficulty in working on *Some Like It Hot*; at Yves Montand for treating casually in person and in print an affair she had hoped would replace her disintegrating marriage to Miller; and at Miller himself for his inability to make her feel secure and for creating a role she felt was one more variation on a dumb blonde.

Lena Pepitone described Marilyn's unhappiness with that role in *Misfits*, particularly the way she persuades Clark Gable and his friends not to sell for killing the wild horses they have just rounded up. "I convince them by throwing a fit, not by explaining anything. So I have a fit. A screaming crazy fit. . . . And to think, *Arthur* did this to me. . . . If that's what he thinks of me, well, then I'm not for him and he's not for me." Fairly or not, she felt used one more time, and perhaps she was. Renée Taylor, who along with Marilyn was one of Lee Strasberg's private students, was impressed with Marilyn's work and called her "a real actress. Not once did I see in a movie—except perhaps *Bus Stop*—the range and talent she demonstrated in class no matter how nervous she was." Taylor recalls her drenched in sweat, so terrified was she of performing live.

Now Marilyn had come to mistrust not only her talent but her own body. It had not produced the child she wanted so badly during her marriage to Arthur Miller. It was beginning to age. She began to fear that she could neither perform roles that didn't depend on her body nor continue to do well in those that did.

In her depression, even money gained a new and symbolic importance. Elizabeth Taylor was getting one million dollars for *Cleopatra* from the same studio that paid Marilyn only $100,000 a picture. She raged about that. In *Something's Got to Give*, a dubious sex comedy that was a price of her return to Hollywood, she wrongly suspected competition from Cyd Charisse, even convincing herself that Charisse was lightening her hair in order to upstage Marilyn. When assured her costar would have darker hair, not blonde, Marilyn said suspiciously, "Her *unconscious* wants it blonde." By now, she told a friend that she also mistrusted Lee Strasberg for his failure to deliver a television project they had planned, and even for his encouragement of her dreams of being a serious actress. After all, her sex films had been far more financially successful than her more serious ones. Perhaps she should have stuck with that security.

Most of all, Marilyn could not overcome the isolation that had been her norm since childhood. Years before, during filming of *All About Eve*, Joe Mankiewicz had observed her on that busy set and on location, eating dinner alone, drinking alone, refusing invitations out of insecurity. "She was not a loner," Mankiewicz observed. "She was just plain *alone*."

She still was. Because she hadn't experienced certainty as a child, she both craved it and seemed unable to create it.

In her attempts to find support and affection, she returned to some echo of the days when, according to her confession to Lena Pepitone, she'd had an early and naïve affair with acting coach Natasha Lytess. "I'd let any guy, or girl, do what they wanted if I thought they were my friend." She went from a public affair with Frank Sinatra to private ones with the still-loyal Joe DiMaggio, with a Mexican screenwriter, perhaps even with her New York masseur and her chauffeur, probably also with men in public life—but none could shore up her fragile sense of self or deliver the security she was missing.

And now, for the first time, even her work was gone. She had been fired from and was trying hard to get rehired for a sex comedy, the very kind of movie she once tried to put behind her. Along with many published rumors that she had become simply unemployable, there were others almost equally hurtful once her last movie was shut down. Norman Rosten, a New York poet who welcomed Marilyn into his family and remained her friend for the last seven years of her life, wrote about "rumors of her coworkers bitterly blaming Marilyn for taking away their jobs. This reaction deeply wounded her," Rosten explained. "She had always felt a strong kinship with working people, from the taxi driver to the grip man on the set; she felt they were her friends, and now they were publicly accusing her of betraying them."

As her interview with George Barris made clear, she was fighting against such "lies" and the media that was publishing them. "Those whom she trusted, the media people who always defended her, were ready to dethrone her," Norman Rosten explained. "Marilyn was down, the count had begun."

In the weeks after her death, there were many public testimonies to her talent and magic. Even Darryl Zanuck, her former boss at Twentieth Century-Fox who had been skeptical of her talents, said, "Nobody discovered her; she earned her own way to stardom."

If Marilyn had been able to write the script, she would have thanked ordinary moviegoers. "I want to say that the people—if I am a star—the people made me a star," she said many times in many ways, "no studio, no person, but the people did."

"Nobody's ever gonna marry me now, Lena. What good
am I? I can't have kids. I can't cook. I've been divorced
three times. Who would want me?"
"Millions of men," I answered.
"Yeah, but who would love me? Who?"

—conversation between Marilyn Monroe
and Lena Pepitone

In 1957, Dalia Leeds, a young Israeli woman who had married an American and moved to New York, began taking her newborn son for an outing each day near her apartment. On a bench in the small park at the end of East Fifty-seventh Street, she often noticed a solitary woman wearing sunglasses, a kerchief over hair curlers, and, in spite of the spring weather, a fur coat over jeans. Unlike other regulars there, she didn't bring a book or a child or a friend. She just sat watching the children play.

After a few days, the woman introduced herself to Dalia as "Mrs. Miller" and asked if she could hold the baby. A stranger wanting to hold her son seemed peculiar at first, but Mrs. Miller was shy and gentle. Soon they had struck up an odd friendship, and chatted each day about children, New York, and their mutual feelings of being a little alone. Dalia's temporary isolation in a new country, speaking a foreign language, seemed to connect to a permanent shyness and loneliness in her American friend.

"She talked mostly about children," Dalia remembered some thirty years later. "She was very curious about being pregnant, about what you fed a child, how you diapered it—everything. She wondered if I got bored just sitting there, being a mother, and I explained that I always brought a book to the park. When she discovered that I also went to school in the afternoons, she wanted to know who took care of the baby and how I could do both. I explained about baby-sitters. We laughed about having six children. She never confided in me about what difficulties she was having, but she very much wanted to have a child.

"I invited her to my house for coffee, but she never came. She would just ask each day if she would see me tomorrow. Even after the other mothers there realized that this was Marilyn Monroe—her voice gave her away, I think, or just taking off her sunglasses—we tried to respect her privacy. She would play with the kids, hold them in her lap, and they adored having her. I think the park became a cozy place for her.

"One day in June, she told me that she wanted me to know I wouldn't be seeing her. She was going away for the summer with her husband, and hoped she would come back the next year—but she never did. I decided I would never trust gossip magazines again—she was so

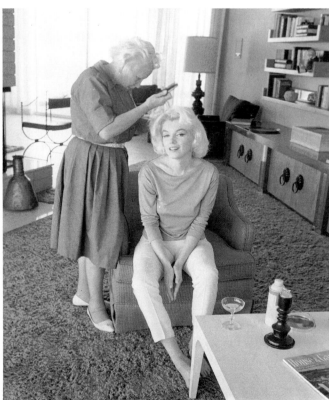

Barris photographed hairdresser Agnes Flanagan and make-up man Whitey Snyder with Marilyn in the summer of 1962. "If anything happens to me," a twenty-seven-year-old Marilyn had asked Snyder almost a decade earlier, "promise me you'll make me up." After her death, fortified with gin and friendship, Snyder fulfilled that promise.

different from her image. Not a sexpot, not glamorous, but just an ordinary woman who was shy, curious, and lonely."

Because she was responding to another human being, not to celebrity or symbols, there is a trustworthiness about the impressions of this thoughtful young Israeli. There is also an honesty about Marilyn's attitude toward an unknown woman she could easily have impressed by revealing her public identity, but chose instead to learn from. Indeed, Marilyn seemed to value and be fascinated by encounters with women who were not competitive or sexually jealous of her, and therefore could be used as friends and teachers. Lena Pepitone, a young Italian woman whom she employed as a maid in New York in the fall of that same year, described in her memoir Marilyn's odd combination of friendship, curiosity, and envy, and her constant questioning and interest in Lena's two sons, her husband, her daily life, her family in Italy—everything. Marilyn seemed to be trying desperately to learn how to live in a family, to have friends, to be a wife and mother, and still have another identity; to be an ordinary woman. Perhaps because she had been deprived of mothering, which is the deepest way all of us learn as children about what a female human being can be, this basic knowledge was what Marilyn hungered for most. But she also had been deprived of any primary connection in her earliest years, and so constantly looked for someone to cure the past. Since only we can do that for ourselves, Marilyn's search usually began with impossibly high hopes and ended in disillusionment.

There were always women to whom Marilyn looked for learning and protection. But she turned to men more. Objectively, they were more powerful in the world. Subjectively, a totally absent father could be more idealized than a semi-present and very disillusioning mother. Nonetheless, women were her nurturers. Grace McKee, her legal guardian and the most consistent person in her childhood, made extraordinary sacrifices for a little girl who was only the daughter of a friend. Marilyn writes with love and empathy about "my Aunt Grace" in her unfinished autobiography, and especially appreciates her taking on the legal responsibility, against all advice from her friends, for a little girl whose "heritage" was very suspect once her real mother had entered a mental institution. Perhaps because of those high expectations, Marilyn felt betrayed by the teenage marriage Grace arranged for her in some combination of desperation and goodwill. Years later, Marilyn told several friends that she had borne a son as the result of a rape by a foster father, and that Grace had forced her to give up the baby for adoption. Whether that story was true or a parable made up by Marilyn to express Norma Jeane's emotion of being sexually exploited and emotionally deprived, it is significant that Grace—who did her best, but could not turn the clock back and become a rescuing mother—is described as the betrayer.

Marilyn could also be overly grateful for small favors and kindnesses from women. Even the head of the orphanage, where she had felt abandoned and used like a servant, was remembered with lifelong gratitude for putting powder on the little girl's face and telling her she had lovely skin—a motherly attention for which Norma Jeane was starving. Only Ana Lower, however, the elderly, childless woman whose gentle faith and loving acceptance had been lavished on Norma Jeane as a teenager, and who remained a presence in Marilyn's life until she died in 1948, really met Marilyn's standard for unconditional love. Marilyn never forgot or failed to praise this Aunt Ana who was almost the only member of her chosen family whom Marilyn never rejected. But later, no one, woman or man, was able to support Marilyn enough to satisfy the neediness of the past Norma Jeane.

Ethel Dougherty, the mother-in-law with whom she lived when her husband, Jim Dougherty, first joined the merchant marine, was a temporary refuge, but she expected Norma Jeane to play a wifely role for which the young girl was far from ready. Emmeline Snively, the head of her first modeling agency, was a professional mentor; but, perhaps understandably, she limited herself to that. Several women agents took risks and helped Marilyn at the beginning of her career, but women were not the most powerful figures in Hollywood. Some of the starlets who were her contemporaries might have been her friends, but Marilyn had a hard time overcoming her isolation from peers. They may have been put off by her neediness as well as the problem of competing for parts. Shelley Winters remembers the early Marilyn as a "shy, very pretty blonde girl [who] used to sit in the corner and watch us working actresses at lunch. Her name was Norma Jeane Something. She rarely spoke to us, and when she did, she would whisper. We would shout back at her, 'What did you say?' and that would scare her more. She always wore halter dresses one size too small and carried around a big library book like a dictionary or encyclopedia." Even when Shelley Winters was Marilyn's roommate for a brief period, her extreme insecurity was both an appeal for help and a burden. "When you went to the john," Shelley explained, "she'd think you'd disappeared and she'd been left alone. She'd open up the door to see if you were still there. She was a little child."

Natasha Lytess, Marilyn's acting coach in her early Hollywood years, was a mentor and mother figure. She regarded Marilyn as a piece of clay to be molded, and even took her to live in her home with her young daughter, but she pinned her own professional hopes so firmly to Marilyn that her pupil's independence didn't seem to be her goal. According to rumors of the time as well as Lena Pepitone's memory of a confession by Marilyn, Lytess may have loved and tried to possess her sexually as well. "Marilyn had looked up to her," Lena explained in her own memoirs, "and when she made her advances, Marilyn simply accepted them as part of her training. . . . Marilyn needed to be loved—by anyone who was sincere." As Lena remembered Marilyn saying, "I let Natasha, but that was wrong. She wasn't like a guy. You know, just have a good time and that's that. She got really jealous about the men I

saw, everything. She thought she was my husband. She was a great teacher, but that part of it ruined things for us. I got scared of her, had to get away."

Even as a star, Marilyn appealed to the protective instincts of women as well as men. Jane Russell, Marilyn's costar in *Gentlemen Prefer Blondes*, described her as "a dreamy girl. She's the kind liable to show up with one red shoe and one black shoe. . . . I'd find out when we'd take a break at eleven that she hadn't had any breakfast and forgot she was hungry until I reminded her. She once got her life so balled up that the studio hired a full-time secretary-maid for her. So Marilyn soon got the secretary as balled up as she was and she ended up waiting on the secretary instead of vice versa."

This difficulty in exerting authority over her own life, much less over others, is one that many women have experienced. A lack of self-confidence, a feeling of being unsuited to power, is the emotional training that helps to keep any less-than-equal group in its place. Because Marilyn was disorganized and vulnerable in the extreme, she exaggerated a "femininity" that appealed to men's sexuality and women's protectiveness. Natalie Wood said of Marilyn as an actress, "When you look at Marilyn on the screen, you don't want anything bad to happen to her. You really care that she should be all right . . . happy." As Dame Sybil Thorndike, who acted with Marilyn and Laurence Olivier in *The Prince and the Showgirl*, said, "She has an innocence which is so extraordinary, whatever she plays, however brazen a hussy, it always comes out as an innocent girl. I remember Sir Laurence saying one day during the filming: 'Look at that face—she could be five years old.' "

That very childlike quality gave her the license to upset marriages. Her focus on Yves Montand at the expense of his wife, Simone Signoret, was not the first time Marilyn had decided that a particular woman was not "worthy" of a man, and thus had gone after him with no guilt.

But Marilyn had a protective side, too. She tried to keep others, especially women who were not sexual competitors, from feeling as hurt or abandoned as she had been. When she was asked to pose for photographs in front of Betty Grable's dressing-room door in a publicity effort to present her as the successor to Grable, she refused. Marilyn didn't want to be hurtful by making Grable feel that she was finished. When the press tried to drum up a feud between Marilyn Monroe and Jane Russell as rival sex goddesses, they both remained friendly and supportive of each other. When the Mocambo, an important Los Angeles nightclub, was reluctant to hire a black singer named Ella Fitzgerald, Marilyn "personally called the owner," as Ella Fitzgerald remembers gratefully, "and told him she wanted me booked immediately, and if he would do it, she would take a front table every night. She told him—and it was true, due to Marilyn's superstar status—that the press would go wild. The owner said yes, and Marilyn was there, front table, every night. . . . After that, I never had to play a small jazz club again."

She was also generous in a spontaneous way to people like Lee and Paula Strasberg, whose work she helped support, and to Lena Pepitone, on whom she pressed lavish gifts of cash, money for a warm winter coat, and holidays for Lena's family at Arthur Miller's Connecticut farmhouse. She gave personal gifts to hairdressers and others who worked for her, even making sure to keep Chivas Regal on hand for the cleaning woman. She played big sister to the Rostens' daughter, Patricia, and introduced her to looking prettier with makeup, much as the head of the orphanage had once done for Norma Jeane. Indeed, Norman Rosten's poems for his daughter impressed Marilyn so much that she modified her earlier obsession with having a son. "Thanks the most for your book of poetry—which I spent all Sunday morning in bed with," she wrote to Rosten. "I used to think if I had ever had a child I would have wanted only a son—but after *Songs for Patricia*—I know I would have loved a little girl as

much—but maybe the former feeling was only Freudian anyway. . . ." In her will, Marilyn left money to be used for Patricia's education.

After her marriage to Miller was over and she had returned to California, her last psychiatrist, Dr. Ralph Greenson, invited Marilyn to a birthday party for his daughter, Joan, to whom Marilyn was also becoming an older sister. "Surprise for our guests: Marilyn was invited and she came!" Dr. Greenson told Norman Rosten, who recorded his story. "After an initial shock, several boys took turns dancing with her," Greenson went on, "and soon all of them were on line. It didn't look too promising for the local girls. And no one was dancing anymore with an especially attractive black girl who, until Marilyn arrived, had been the most popular on the floor. Marilyn noticed this, and went over to her. 'You know,' she said, 'you do a step I'd love to do, but don't think I know how. Would you teach it to me?' Then she turned to the others and called out, 'Everybody stop for a few minutes! I'm going to learn a new step.' Now, the point is, Marilyn knew the step, but she let this girl teach it to her. She understood the loneliness of others."

Norman Rosten himself remembered Marilyn's concern when she came to pick him up at a Los Angeles hotel where he was staying on a business trip and found him "chatting with an attractive girl at the switchboard. She brought up the subject later. 'I want you to stay away from that girl,' she said. 'You're happily married.' I glowered in my Humphrey Bogart manner: 'So what about it?' She said, 'So don't go flirting with these chicks. I'll call your wife.' She was serious. She had this protectiveness toward women she liked." And Marilyn liked Rosten's wife, Hedda, a lot.

As Ella Fitzgerald concluded, "She was an unusual woman—a little ahead of her times. And she didn't know it."

But Marilyn was also a woman of the fifties. She took women as a group no more seriously than she took herself, and only connected with the same kind of problems that many men of that era would also take seriously: race discrimination, loneliness, poverty. Her empathy with strong women, and her willingness to develop strength in herself, was blocked by her assumptions of what a woman should be. "A woman needs to . . . well, to *support* a man, emotionally I mean," Marilyn explained often, in different ways. "And a man needs to be strong. This is partly what it means to be masculine or feminine. I think it's terribly important to feel feminine, to act feminine. . . . Men need women to be feminine." This belief gave her a dangerous permission to remain dependent that even her various psychiatrists may have reinforced. Apparently they did not challenge Freudian assumptions of female passivity, penis envy, and the like. "I will not discuss psychoanalysis, except to say that I believe in the Freudian interpretation," Marilyn explained. She added, with an irony she couldn't have known, "I hope at some future time to make a glowing report on the wonders that psychiatrists can do for you."

When she did accept authority in women, especially on "unfeminine" matters, she seemed to do so with pleasure and surprise. Marilyn once enrolled in an art and literature course at UCLA in her despair over being uneducated. "The teacher was a woman," she noted. "I was depressed by this at first because I didn't think a woman could teach me anything. But in a few days I knew differently. She was one of the most exciting human beings I had ever met. She talked about the Renaissance and made it sound ten times more important than the Studio's biggest epic. I drank in everything she said." But when her association with such women was longer, they ran the risk of becoming mother figures who were objects of nearly impossible hunger and expectation. Paula Strasberg, the wife of acting teacher Lee Strasberg, was her on-set acting coach during Marilyn's later movies. For better or worse, she seems to have tried to supply undiluted and even uncritical support. Olivier, who also directed *The Prince and the Showgirl*, insisted that he personally heard Paula telling Marilyn, "You haven't yet any idea of the importance of your position in the world. You are the greatest woman of your time, the greatest human being of your time, of any time—you name it. You can't think of anybody, I mean—no, not even Jesus—except you're more popular." Olivier concluded that "Paula knew nothing; she was no actress, no director, no teacher, no adviser, except in Marilyn's eyes. For she had one talent: she could butter Marilyn up." If he was right, Marilyn's need for a champion on the set may have deprived her of real teaching. Nonetheless, Dame Sybil Thorndike defended Marilyn's talent and ability: "We need her desperately. She's the only one of us who really knows how to act in front of a camera."

Whatever the professional worth of the support Paula supplied, she was finally banished when she was unable to negotiate Marilyn back into her role in *Something's Got to Give*, the last and unfinished film, from which Marilyn was humiliatingly fired.

From the beginning to the end of her life, Marilyn also had a defensive fear of women who were jealous of her: classmates who had snubbed her for being more attractive to boys, Hollywood matrons who jealously guarded their husbands, or actresses like Joan Crawford who first offered Marilyn condescending advice on deportment and clothes, then criticized her publicly as unladylike when she didn't take it. Even Berneice Miracle, Gladys's daughter by her first marriage and Marilyn's lost half sister, was seen as competitive in a different way. Though Marilyn was ecstatic over meeting this unknown relative when they finally found each other in the 1950s, she also felt Berneice had had the advantage of being raised with her real father. "At least you lived with relatives," Marilyn said to her when Berneice talked of difficulties in her childhood.

By the very end of Marilyn's life, there were only two women she was close to and saw regularly: Patricia Newcomb, her press assistant who was also a friend and surrogate younger sister, and Jeanne Carmen, an actress neighbor to whom Marilyn confessed her troubles with insomnia, with work, with men. Even now, Patricia Newcomb continues to guard Marilyn's privacy, and Jeanne Carmen, interviewed recently for a British television special on Marilyn's death, still wondered with tears in her eyes whether she could have saved Marilyn's life by visiting her that last evening.

Of the women whom Marilyn knew as a very young child, her mother's mother died in a mental hospital; her own mother has spent most of her life institutionalized as well; Ana Lower died of a stroke (although Marilyn apparently believed she died of malnutrition); and Grace McKee died a suicide. The teachers of her earliest lessons on femaleness offered life examples that were sad or tragic.

But Marilyn was also shaped by forces that are still familiar, and that were even stronger in the 1950s.

As with most women, the decision to have or not have children was the major undercurrent of her life. It was not easy for young women of the 1950s to resist the pressure to be mothers early—not even technically easy, with no pill, no legal abortion, and no tradition of expecting men to be responsible for contraception. There is strength in the fact that Marilyn resisted that pressure, and at least tried to give birth to herself; there is sadness in her inability to have a child when that was finally possible within a marriage and within Marilyn's own life as an actress. Would raising a child have helped to heal the wounded Norma Jeane inside? Had Marilyn been nurtured enough to nurture a child? She herself wasn't sure. "I've got to make some decisions soon," Marilyn had told Norman Rosten while she was still married to Arthur Miller. "Should I do my next picture or stay home and try to have a baby again? That's what I want most of all, the baby, I guess, but maybe God is trying to tell me something, I mean with all my pregnancy problems. I'd probably make a kooky mother, I'd love my child to death. I want it, yet I'm scared."

Whatever the right answer for her may have been, Marilyn was never allowed to find out.

The fifties also shaped her public life. Even Jean Harlow had been allowed more toughness and self-direction in the postsuffrage freedom of the 1920s and 1930s, but Marilyn was rewarded for the childlike compliance, and the big-breasted beauty that symbolized women's return to home, hearth, childbearing, and togetherness after World War II. Then, women who had tasted independence in the wartime work force were being encouraged to go home and let returning veterans have the jobs; to have children to make up for wartime losses; to be consumers of peacetime goods and keep the factories going. Marilyn was made into a symbol of what a postwar woman should be.

Yet inside all that artifice, there was a unique combination of vulnerability and strength, talent and desperation, fragility and a refusal to give up. If Marilyn Monroe had been easy to imitate, there would have been many more of her by now—and there are none.

Perhaps she wasn't an actress at all. Perhaps her unique magic—especially the empathy she inspired in women—came from a different kind of talent. "She went right down into her own personal experience for everything, reached down and pulled something out of herself that was unique and extraordinary," explained John Huston, who directed her. "She had no techniques. It was all the truth, it was only Marilyn. But it was Marilyn, plus. She found things, found things about womankind in herself."

FATHERS AND LOVERS

"I'm just mad about men. If only there was someone special."

—*Marilyn Monroe*

Even when she was unknown, and certainly after she became an international sex goddess, Marilyn Monroe had the good luck and the bad luck to cross paths with a surprising number of the world's most powerful men. The fragile framework of her life was almost obscured by the heavy ornaments of their names. For those many people who have been more interested in the famous men than in Marilyn, her story often has become a voyeuristic excuse. Like a gossip column:

★★★★★★★

Marilyn's career began when she was discovered by an Army photographer assigned "to take morale-building shots of pretty girls" in a defense plant for *Yank* and *Stars and Stripes* magazines and Marilyn was a pretty eighteen-year-old worker on the assembly line. That photographer's commanding officer, a young captain who spent World War II supervising this kind of morale-building work from his desk in a movie studio, was **Ronald Reagan**.

★★★★★★★

More pinup shots of Marilyn were published in magazines like *Laff* and *Titter*, and they caught the attention of **Howard Hughes**, the actress-collecting head of RKO Studios, as he lay in a hospital recovering from a flying accident. A gossip column report that he had "instructed an aide to sign her for pictures" encouraged a rival studio, Twentieth Century-Fox, to sign her as a starlet. It probably also led to a date between Hughes and Marilyn, from which she emerged with her face rubbed raw by his beard, and the gift of a pin that, she was surprised to learn later, was worth only five hundred dollars.

★★★★★★★

Marilyn was paid fifty dollars for the nude calendar shots she did under another name, but just one was bought for five hundred dollars once she was an actress and had been identified as the model. The purchaser was an unknown young editor named **Hugh Hefner**, and that nude greatly increased the appeal of the first issue of *Playboy*. (A year after her death, nude photos taken on the set during her swimming scene in *Something's Got to Give*, her last and unfinished film, would increase *Playboy*'s sales again.) An original copy of that historic nude calendar also hung in the home of **J. Edgar Hoover**. Though he accumulated an FBI file on Marilyn, Hoover, whose only known

---

Facing page: George Barris photographed Marilyn at the thank-you party she gave for cast and friends of *The Seven Year Itch*. He remembered: "Everyone wanted to be near her, to touch her."

companion for forty years was a male aide, proudly displayed this nude calendar to guests. Originals of that calendar continue to sell for up to two hundred dollars each. For years, a well-known pornographic movie called *Apple Knockers and the Coke Bottle* was also sold on the premise that Marilyn was the actress in it—but she was not.

★★★★★★★★

Of the two most popular male idols of the 1950s, **Joe DiMaggio** and **Frank Sinatra**, she married one and had an affair with the other. Of the two most respected actors, **Marlon Brando** and **Laurence Olivier**, she had an affair and long-term friendship with the first and costarred with and was directed by the second. She played opposite such stars as **Clark Gable**, **Montgomery Clift**, **Tony Curtis**, and **Jack Lemmon**, and was directed by some illustrious directors: **John Huston**, **Joe Mankiewicz**, **Fritz Lang**, **Otto Preminger**, **Billy Wilder**, and **Joshua Logan**. She costarred and fell in love with Europe's most popular singing star, **Yves Montand**. She married one of the most respected American playwrights, **Arthur Miller**, and acted in a film he wrote for her.

★★★★★★★★

When **Prince Rainier of Monaco** was looking for a wife to carry on the royal line, **Aristotle Onassis** thought Monaco's fading tourism might be boosted if the new princess were also glamorous and famous. He asked **George Schlee**, longtime consort of **Greta Garbo**, for suggestions. Schlee asked **Gardner Cowles**, scion of the publishing family and publisher of *Look* magazine, who came up with the name of Marilyn Monroe. Cowles actually hosted a dinner where Marilyn, newly divorced from **Joe DiMaggio**, and Schlee were guests, and Marilyn said she would be happy to meet the Prince ("Prince Reindeer," as she jokingly called him). But plans for "Princess Marilyn" were cut short when Prince Rainier announced his engagement to **Grace Kelly**. Marilyn phoned Grace with friendly congratulations: "I'm so glad you've found a way out of this business."

★★★★★★★★

The CIA may have considered using an acquaintance between Marilyn and **President Sukarno of Indonesia** for foreign-policy purposes. In 1956, at Sukarno's request, she had been invited to a diplomatic dinner during his visit to California. He was clearly taken with her. There were rumors that they saw each other afterward, though Sukarno, who liked to brag about his sexual conquests, didn't brag about Marilyn. Later, when a coup against his regime in Indonesia seemed imminent, Marilyn tried unsuccessfully to persuade poet Norman Rosten and Arthur Miller, by then her husband, to "rescue" Sukarno by offering him a personal invitation of refuge here. "We're letting a sweet man go down the drain," she protested, with characteristic loyalty to anyone in trouble. "Some country this is." In 1958, according to a CIA officer in Asia, there was a plan to bring Marilyn and Sukarno together in order to make him more favorable to the United States, but the plan was never fulfilled.

★★★★★★★★

At the 1959 American National Exhibition in Moscow, a close-up of Marilyn in *Some Like It Hot* was shown on sixteen giant movie screens simultaneously, and applauded by forty thousand Soviet viewers each day. When **Premier Nikita Khrushchev** made his famous visit here later that year and Marilyn was one of the stars invited to a large Hollywood luncheon for him, he seemed to seek her out. Other introductions waited while he held Marilyn's hand and told her, "You're a very lovely young lady." She answered: "My husband, Arthur Miller, sends you his greetings. There should be more of this kind of thing. It would help both our countries understand each other." Though Marilyn refused to disclose this exchange, it was overheard and published. As she was boarding the plane to New York, the reporters applauded her, as if thanking her for thawing the Cold War a little. Marilyn was very touched by that. "Khrushchev looked at me," she later said proudly, "like a man looks at a woman."

★★★★★★★★

As part of her quest for education, Marilyn sought out writers and intellectuals: **Truman Capote** and **Carl Sandburg** were among her acquaintances. (She was "a beautiful child" to Capote. Sandburg said: "She was not the usual movie idol. There was something democratic about her. She was the type who would join in and wash up the supper dishes even if you didn't ask her.") As part of their quest for popularity, writers and intellectuals sought out Marilyn. **Drew Pearson**, the most powerful of Washington columnists, got her to write a guest column in the summer of 1954. **Edward R. Murrow** chose her for one of his coveted televised "Person to Person" interviews. **Lee Strasberg**, serious, Stanislavsky-trained guru of the Actors Studio, took her on as a pupil, ranked her talent with that of Marlon Brando, and seemed impressed by her fame. ("The greatest tragedy was that people, even my father in a way, took advantage of her," said his son, John Strasberg. "They glommed onto her special sort of life, her special characteristics, when what she needed was love.")

★★★★★★★★

Another writer and intellectual who wanted to meet Marilyn was **Norman Mailer**. "One of the frustrations of his life," Mailer explained, characteristically referring to himself in the third person in *Marilyn*, the biography of her he wrote a decade after her death, "was that he had never met her. . . . The secret ambition, after all, had been to steal Marilyn; in all his vanity he thought no one was so well-suited to bring out the best in her as himself. . . ." In this lengthy "psychohistory" of Marilyn, he finds significance in the fact that her name was an (imperfect) anagram of his, and describes her as "a lover of books who did not read . . . a giant and an emotional pygmy . . . a sexual oven whose fire may rarely have been lit. . . ." What he does not say is that Marilyn did not want to meet him. Although—or perhaps because—she had read his work, she refused several of Mailer's efforts to set up a meeting, "formal or otherwise," through their mutual friend, **Norman Rosten**. "She resisted his approach," wrote Rosten. "She was 'busy,' or she 'had nothing to say,' or 'he's too tough.' " Under Rosten's continuing pressure, she finally issued Mailer an invitation to a party—at a time when he couldn't come—but nothing more private. Though Mailer quotes from Rosten's slender book about Marilyn, he omits the account of his own rejection.

★★★★★★★★

Marilyn was flattered by attention from serious men, but she also had standards. "Some of those bastards in Hollywood wanted me to drop Arthur, said it would ruin my career," she explained after her public support and private financial aid with legal fees had helped **Arthur Miller** survive investigation by the House Committee on Un-American Activities. "They're born cowards and want you to be like them. One reason I want to see **Kennedy** win is that **Nixon's** associated with that whole scene." While in Mexico, where she went in the last months of her life to buy furnishings for her new home in Los Angeles, she met **Fred Vanderbilt Field**, a member of the wealthy Vanderbilt family and known as "America's foremost silver-spoon Communist," who was living there in exile. He and his wife found her "warm, attractive, bright, and witty; curious about things, people, and ideas—also incredibly complicated. . . . She told us of her strong feelings about civil rights, for black equality, as well as her admiration for what was being done in China, her anger at red-baiting and McCarthyism, and her hatred of **J. Edgar Hoover**."

★★★★★★★★

As an actress, she often objected to playing a "dumb blonde," which she feared would also be her fate in real life, but she might have accepted the "serious actress" appeal of playing Cecily, a patient of **Sigmund Freud**. After all, the director of this movie was **John Huston** and the screenwriter was **Jean-Paul Sartre**, who considered Marilyn "one of the greatest actresses alive." Ironically, **Dr. Ralph Greenson**, a well-known

Freudian who was Marilyn's analyst in the last months of her life, advised against it, because, he said, Freud's daughter did not approve of the film. Otherwise, Marilyn would have been called upon to enact the psychotic fate she feared most in real life, and to play the patient of a man whose belief in female passivity may have been part of the reason she was helped so little by psychiatry.

★★★★★★★★

The paths of these men in Marilyn's life also crossed in odd ways. **Robert Mitchum**, Marilyn's costar in *River of No Return*, had worked next to her first husband, **Jim Dougherty**, at an aircraft factory, and heard him discuss his wife, Norma Jeane. **Elia Kazan**, with whom Marilyn once had an affair, later directed *After the Fall*, **Arthur Miller**'s play that was based on his marriage to Marilyn. At a post-play party, Kazan and Miller could be heard comparing intimate notes on Marilyn while being served supper by **Barbara Loden**, the young actress who played the part of Marilyn and to whom Kazan was later married.

★★★★★★★★

Most famous of all these famous men was **Jack Kennedy**, with whom Marilyn was linked both before and during his presidency, and **Bobby Kennedy**, with whom she was linked while he was attorney general. In the absence of the rare and unwonted witness to an affair, the evidence to most private romances is hearsay or one-sided. But Marilyn told many friends of both affairs, and was seen at parties, arriving and leaving hotels, on the beach at Malibu with Jack, and at the home of Kennedy brother-in-law **Peter Lawford** with Bobby. The unanswered questions about her death, books and televisions shows on possible conspiracies, right-wing and left-wing motives for her "murder"—these have assured that Marilyn's name will be linked with the Kennedys for all the years she is remembered. Partly because of them, there seems to be more interest in her death than in her life.

Marilyn appealed to these men who were friends and strangers, husbands and lovers, colleagues and teachers, for many different reasons: some wanted to sexually conquer her, others to sexually protect her. Some hoped to absorb her wisdom, while others were amused by her innocence; many basked in the glory of her public image, but others dreamed of keeping her at home. "She is the most womanly woman I can imagine," Arthur Miller said before their marriage. ". . . Most men become more of what they are around her: a phony becomes more phony, a confused man becomes more confused, a retiring man more retiring. She's kind of a lodestone that draws out of the male animal his essential qualities."

Norman Mailer's opinion was even more sweeping. She "was every man's love affair with America," he explained in *Marilyn*. ". . . The men who knew the most about love would covet her, and the classical pimples of the adolescent working his first gas pump would also pump for her. . . . Marilyn suggested sex might be difficult and dangerous with others, but ice cream with her." She was a magical, misty screen on which every fantasy could be projected without discipline or penalty, because no clear image was already there.

What Marilyn and the real Norma Jeane inside her wanted from men was much more limited and clear, but almost as magical, as what they expected from her. She hoped to learn, not to teach; to gain seriousness not sacrifice it; to trust completely but not to be completely trustworthy; to be protected "inside" while a man took on the world "outside"; to be younger, never older; to be the child and not the parent. In short, she looked to men for the fathering—and perhaps the mothering—that she had never had. She didn't want the mutual support of a partnership, but the unconditional, one-sided support given to a child.

Jim Dougherty was very aware of his role. When Norma Jeane was told about her illegitimacy before their marriage, she determined to get in touch with her real father—the handsome, idealized man she had known only as a photograph.

"This is Norma Jeane," Jim remembered her saying in a tremulous voice when she finally got the courage to phone the fantasy stranger she had dreamed of all her childhood. "I'm Gladys's daughter."

"Then she slumped and put the receiver back," Dougherty wrote in his memoir of their marriage. " 'Oh, honey!' she said. 'He hung up on me!'

"After that incident," he explained, "I'd say we were closer than ever. I was her lover, husband, and father, the whole tamale. And when my leave had just about run out and I was getting ready to return to the ship, it was another very emotional experience for her. . . . Each time I left it was a destructive thing that hit her extremely hard. She wanted something, *someone* that she could hold onto all the time. If we were out together, even at the movies, she had a tight grip on my arm or my hand."

Throughout their marriage, Marilyn called her young husband "Daddy." Jim's trips with the merchant marine were not just the sad absences of a partner, but traumatic desertions by a parent. Without those long trips the marriage might have lasted for the reason that many once did: the wife had neither the financial nor the emotional ability to leave. But once she felt deserted, Norma Jeane turned to work in the defense plant where she was to be "discovered"; to brief affairs with other men for warmth and security; and to modeling and acting as a way of living in her fantasies for a few minutes or hours at a time. She felt emotionally separated long before the divorce papers were signed.

When Marilyn fell in love for what she described as the first time, the man was even more clearly a father figure. Freddy Karger was a musician employed by movie studios to do vocal coaching (he was Marilyn's teacher); a divorced man raising his son (he was not only older but literally a father); a dark, handsome, compact man (like the man in the photograph); and a part of an unusually close household that included his mother, his divorced sister, his sister's two children, and his own son, all of whom took Marilyn into their hearts (a ready-made family). Indeed, there was the added seduction of the Karger family's home as a kind of Hollywood salon where anyone from Valentino to Jack Pickford had gathered. It contrasted painfully with Marilyn's life as a starlet eating on as little as a dollar a day and living in a lonely furnished room. When Karger first brought Marilyn home to dinner, he said to his mother, "This is a little girl who is very lonely and broke." Marilyn felt taken care of. She fell in love.

Unfortunately, Karger seemed to feel only some combination of sexual attraction and pity for Marilyn—not love. He was almost as rejecting as her absent father had been. She was no masochist in her relationships with men—if anything, she exacted an impossible degree of loyalty and support—but in her obsession for first love and first family combined, she accepted almost anything.

"I knew he liked me and was happy to be with me," Marilyn wrote, "but his love didn't seem anything like mine. He criticized my mind. He kept pointing out how little I knew and how unaware of life I was. It was sort of true. I tried to know more by reading books. I had a new friend, Natasha Lytess. She was an acting coach and a woman of deep culture. She told me what to read. I read Tolstoy and Turgenev. They excited me, and I couldn't lay a book down till I'd finished it. . . . But I didn't feel my mind was improving."

" 'You cry too easily,' he'd say. 'That's because your mind isn't developed. Compared to your breasts it's embryonic.' I couldn't contradict him because I had to look up that word in a dictionary. 'Your mind is inert,' he'd say. 'You never think about life. You just float through it on that pair of water wings you wear.' "

But the final insult came when Karger said he couldn't marry her because, should anything happen to him, his son would be left with her. "It wouldn't be right for him to be brought up by a woman like you," Marilyn remembered Karger saying. Given the child inside herself and her special kinship with children, that was the ultimate cruelty.

"A man can't love a woman for whom he feels contempt," Marilyn explained. "He can't love her if his mind is ashamed of her." She tried to leave Freddy Karger but couldn't stay away. ("It's hard to do something that hurts your heart," Marilyn wrote movingly, "especially when it's a new heart and you think that one hurt may kill it.") When she finally left for good, Karger, at least in Marilyn's memory, suddenly became more interested—but it was too late.

"I was torn myself and wondered, Could it work?" Karger later said. "Her ambition bothered me to a great extent. I wanted a woman who was a homebody. She might have thrown it all over for the right man."

She did remain friends for the rest of her life with Freddy's mother, Anne Karger, just as she later would remain close to Joe DiMaggio's son, to Arthur Miller's children and his father, Isadore Miller, long after she was divorced from those two husbands. One of the consistencies of her life was this habit of attaching herself to other people's families: to Natasha Lytess and her daughter; to Lee and Paula Strasberg and their two children; to poet Norman Rosten, his wife, Hedda, and their daughter; to photographer Milton Greene and his wife, Amy; to Dr. Ralph Greenson, his wife and two children, who took her in as part of her treatment—to every friendly home that crossed her path. The life-style and relatives that came with a particular man seemed to attract her more, and to survive longer, than the man himself.

Freddy Karger added another association to the gossip value of Marilyn's life. In spite of his professed desire for "a homebody," he soon married Jane Wyman, newly divorced from Ronald Reagan and the mother of Maureen and Mike Reagan. Karger and Wyman divorced, remarried, and divorced again. While they were married, Marilyn wrote about Karger without naming him, saying only, "He's married now to a movie star . . . and I wish him well and anybody he loves well."

But having learned a painful lesson of unequal love, Marilyn's next serious affair was a more paternal one. Johnny Hyde, an important agent thirty years her senior, felt much more for Marilyn than she did for him. It was Hyde who helped her get the small but crucial role in John Huston's *The Asphalt Jungle*, who praised her talents to every important producer in Hollywood, and who made sure she was seen at all the right parties.

To Hyde, she confessed the truth of her emotional numbness after Karger, and he listened to her with kindness and understanding. "Kindness is the strangest thing to find in a lover—or in anybody," she wrote about Hyde. "No man had ever looked on me with such kindness. He not only knew me, he knew Norma Jeane, too. He knew all the pain and all the desperate things in me. When he put his arms around me and said he loved me, I knew it was true. Nobody had ever loved me like that. I wished with all my heart that I could love him back. . . . You might as well try to make yourself fly as to make yourself love. But I felt everything else toward Johnny Hyde, and I was always happy to be with him. It was like being with a whole family and belonging to a full set of relatives."

They were an odd couple: a tiny, wizened man considerably shorter than the lush, youthful Marilyn. Later, she would wonder if she had let his looks and age influence her feelings, but she confounded Hollywood cynics by refusing to marry this millionaire who wanted to protect her. She accepted sex without love; at least that brought her the illusion of intimacy. But she drew the line at marriage without love. After Hyde's death, his family tried to bar her from the funeral, and, far worse, Hollywood gossip blamed Hyde's heart attack on his feverish work on Marilyn's career, his constant squiring her to the right parties as well as to the right producers. It was like being accused of killing the father she desperately wanted. Marilyn's fragile sense of self collapsed, and she attempted suicide (at twenty-four, this was, by her own account, her third attempt). Marilyn's suicide note left her two prized possessions, a car and a fur stole, to acting coach Natasha Lytess, and it was she who saved the unconscious Marilyn by emptying her mouth of the purplish paste of sleeping pills and getting help.

This guilt about leaving or killing a father figure was also a recurrent theme in her life. After all, a father, unlike a husband and partner, must be left behind as part of a child's inevitable growth; so to confuse the two is to build in an experience of guilt. Perhaps she had neglected Johnny Hyde during the last month of his life, but she was with him in his last days in the hospital. Seven years later, in 1957, she was still guiltily telling Lena Pepitone, "If I had married him maybe he could have lived. He used to say that I was the only one who could save his life. . . ." In 1960, when Clark Gable died of a heart attack after costarring with Marilyn in *The Misfits*, Marilyn was publicly blamed again—this time for her lateness and drug problems that had dragged out arduous weeks of filming in the harsh Nevada desert. Those rumors following *The Misfits* ended in another suicide attempt by Marilyn, one of more than half a dozen such close calls with self-induced death, both purposeful and accidental. Some seemed to be caused by guilt and others by loneliness, some by leaving and others by being left, and at least one by her inability to bear a child, but all reached down to the buried sense of worthlessness within herself.

Only two recorded incidents betray anger at the father who left her (usually, as her feelings of worthlessness suggested, she somehow felt she deserved to be left). In talking to her longtime friend, columnist Sidney Skolsky, she implicitly admitted she had delayed shooting and kept the whole cast waiting in ways that she knew were physically hard for Gable. "Was I punishing my father?" she wondered aloud to Skolsky. "Getting even for all the years he's kept me waiting?" Earlier, a New York friend remembered Marilyn's shocking response to a party-game request for personal fantasies: she said she imagined disguising herself in a black wig, meeting her father, seducing him, and then asking vindictively, "How do you feel now to have a daughter that you've made love to?"

It's difficult to realize that such dark thoughts could come from the sugary blonde Norman Mailer desired, with her "sweet little rinky-dink of a voice and all the cleanliness of all the clean American backyards. . . . A sweet peach bursting before one's eyes. . . ." Perhaps her need to fulfill this pink-and-white American sex-goddess image was part of the reason she chose Joe DiMaggio for her first lengthy affair after Johnny Hyde, and for the first husband she chose for herself. What better way to gain the love and support she craved than to become the wife of this quiet man whom sportswriters called the "Last Hero"? What could be a better bulwark against her own depressions and insomnia than this handsome stoic who seemed to have no moods?

"I had thought I was going to meet a loud, sporty fellow," Marilyn wrote about their first date. "Instead I found myself smiling at a reserved gentleman in a gray suit. . . . I would have guessed he was either a steel magnate or a congressman." DiMaggio was quiet where Hollywood men were braggers, and yet he still was the center of attention in any gathering. "You learn to be silent and smiling like that from having millions of people look at you with love and excitement while you stand alone," Marilyn noted. When he informed her in his enigmatic way that he didn't mind going out once with a girl, but he didn't like the second date, and seldom lasted for a third, Marilyn took on the challenge.

The courtship lasted two years. With her usual insecurity, Marilyn continued to have affairs with other men in a way that would have infuriated DiMaggio had he known. The marriage itself lasted barely nine months. DiMaggio was a traditional husband who liked to stay home and watch sports, or go out with the boys. Once in possession of Marilyn, he resented her career, disliked the invasion of his own privacy that their marriage brought about, and was angered by both Hollywood's sex-movie use of her body and by any immodest clothes in daily life. Even a low-necked dress could set him off, and Marilyn took to wearing Peter Pan collars and dresses that were her usual skintight style, but exposed little bare skin. When he wrote Marilyn letters, he signed them "Pa."

"I have to be careful writing about my husband Joe DiMaggio because he winces easily," Marilyn later wrote. "Many of the things that seem normal or even desirable to me are very annoying to him." Among those things was Marilyn's love of learning. She could not get Joe to read any of the books she cared about, or any books at all. She tried, in her words, "everything from Mickey Spillane to Jules Verne." On his birthday, she gave him a medal engraved with a quote from *The Little Prince*: "True love is visible not to the eyes, but to the heart, for eyes may be deceived." DiMaggio's mystified response was, "What the hell does that mean?" She longed to be the pupil, yet she had become the teacher of a student who wouldn't learn.

Soon Marilyn's marriage degenerated into a classic struggle between her career or interests and her husband's wishes. For DiMaggio, the marriage sank into a classic conflict between his traditional values and a wife who had a world of her own. His old ulcer acted up. His attempt to isolate Marilyn in his hometown of San Francisco failed. There is some evidence that his anger may have led him to treat her with violence. Natasha Lytess remembered Marilyn phoning "day and night, sometimes in tears, complaining about the way he misused her." Marlon Brando noted once that Marilyn's arm was black and blue. Her friend Amy Greene was shocked to see bruises on Marilyn's back, and Marilyn admitted reluctantly that Joe was the cause. A New York press aide remembers Marilyn phoning her in fear of an angry DiMaggio who could be heard shouting in the background. While they were staying in New York so Marilyn could film *The Seven Year Itch* DiMaggio seemed to alternate between cold distance in public and anger in private. Back in Hollywood, Marilyn announced to her director, Billy Wilder, that she and Joe were getting a divorce.

Whether or not there was real violence, which only DiMaggio knows, his pattern of behavior does resemble that of many battering husbands: traditional values, possessiveness, attempts to cut off his wife's contact with the rest of the world, emotional distance, and anger at disobedience to his wishes. Once he and Marilyn were separated, the second half of the same pattern took over: extreme contrition combined with a firm belief that she still "belonged" to him. Like many such men, he seemed to mistrust what he could possess, and to worship what he could not. DiMaggio began to quiz others about whether or not Marilyn had left him for another man (she had not), had her followed by detectives even after they were legally separated, and stood watching for hours in the shadows outside her doorway. DiMaggio staged a raid on a stranger's apartment—reportedly with the help of his friend Frank Sinatra—because Joe wrongly believed Marilyn was there with a lover. Later, this famous "Wrong Door Raid" led to a successful suit against Joe DiMaggio and Sinatra. Hal Schaefer, a composer and pianist who was Marilyn's friend, coach, and eventually lover in that period, learned to regard DiMaggio with fear. "I was not the cause of the breakup," Schaefer told Monroe biographer Anthony Summers. "It was already broken up, and not because of me. She would have left him no matter what. . . . But DiMaggio couldn't believe that. His ego was such that he couldn't believe that."

Nonetheless, when Marilyn was put in Payne Whitney Clinic in New York for her drug dependency and depression following her breakup with Arthur Miller, she pleaded with Lee and Paula Strasberg to get her out. They did not help—but Joe DiMaggio did. He seems to have understood her panic at being locked up in an institution, as her grandmother and mother had been, and he got her into a hospital where she could get treatment without locked doors and closed wards.

Despite their breakup, he remained jealous. His long friendship with Frank Sinatra was broken when Sinatra and Marilyn had an affair. But once he finally gave up ownership of Marilyn, he also continued to be her friend. They talked on the phone and occasionally saw each other in the years following their divorce. Marilyn spoke of him with affection.

In the end, it was DiMaggio who arranged her funeral. He spent the night before it in a vigil over her casket, and cried openly at the service. He kissed her one last time and said "I love you" over and over again. She was buried with his flowers in her hands.

Arthur Miller was not at the funeral. He had remarried, his wife was expecting a baby, and, as Miller put it, Marilyn was "not really there anymore." Nonetheless, his marriage to Marilyn had been her last and longest. He filled more of the requirements of an idealized father than the Last Hero had done. Though both DiMaggio and Miller were about a decade older than Marilyn, already fathers, dark-haired as Marilyn's father-in-the-photograph had been, and widely admired, Arthur Miller was also able to be a teacher in the cultural sense that mattered to Marilyn, and to support her hopes of being a serious actress. It was a long distance from DiMaggio, a man of few words, to a Pulitzer-winning author, and Marilyn seemed eager to make the journey.

In fact, Marilyn and Miller had first met in 1950 just after her attempted suicide over the death of Johnny Hyde. Together with Elia Kazan, Miller had visited the set of *As Young as You Feel*, a movie featuring Marilyn that was directed by a friend of Kazan's. When they went in search of her, they found her alone in a studio warehouse, weeping over Hyde's death. Miller never forgot that.

That same week they met at a party, sat on a sofa, and talked. He was a quiet, strong, un-Hollywood man who wrote very good plays about very ordinary people, and who took seriously Marilyn's desire to improve herself. She told Natasha Lytess, with whom she was then living, "It was like running into a tree! You know, like a cool drink when you've got a fever." Marilyn never forgot that meeting either.

But Miller was still married then, and they only corresponded briefly. It wasn't until after Marilyn had met, married, and divorced Joe DiMaggio and moved to New York to study acting, that her courtship with Miller really began. She read the books he recommended, practiced cooking, adopted his friends and his country life-style, and began to call him "Art," "Poppy," or "Pa." Miller supported her studies at the Actors Studio, in spite of his misgivings about her growing dependence on the Strasbergs. He was touched by her profound connection to children and to nature, and even defended her sexual way of dressing that DiMaggio had detested. "Miller was in love," wrote his friend Norman Rosten, "completely, seriously, with the ardor of a man released." Before their marriage in the summer of 1956, Marilyn spent a good deal of time learning about Judaism. Miller himself was not religious, but she wanted to be part of his family's tradition. "I'll cook noodles like your mother," she told him on their wedding day. On the back of a wedding photograph, she wrote: "Hope, Hope, Hope."

For Marilyn, the first disillusionment came on their honeymoon trip to London for the long filming of *The Prince and the Showgirl*. She had been having her usual problems with insomnia, lateness, dependence on sleeping pills, and terror of performing. The problems were probably made worse by what she felt was director and costar Laurence Olivier's condescension toward her. He had been warned by Joshua Logan that Marilyn needed support not criticism, but he was critical nonetheless and accused the nervous Marilyn of not even being able to count. Arthur Miller took on the challenging role of shoring up Marilyn's confidence, interpreting her to her colleagues, and just getting her to work: he joined Milton Greene, Marilyn's new partner in Marilyn Monroe Productions, and acting coach Paula Strasberg in a three-way tug of war over her professional life. But Miller was also trying to use this five-month stay in London as a time to write. Marilyn was shocked to find notes about her that Miller had been keeping, as if she herself were only grist for his writerly mill. Furthermore, the notes were very critical.

"It was something about how disappointed he was in me," Marilyn later explained to Lee and Paula Strasberg. "How he thought I was some kind of angel but now he guessed he was wrong. That his first wife had let him down, but I had done something worse. Olivier was beginning to think I was a troublesome bitch and that he [Arthur] no longer had a decent answer to that one."

For Marilyn, who believed that trust had to be total and love unconditional—that to love a man, she had to trust him completely, as a child trusts a parent—this betrayal was unforgivable. For Miller, the content of the note itself betrayed the beginning of his understanding that her flattering, childlike, worshipful attitude had a terrible cause.

The first bloom was off their marriage when they returned, but they managed a fairly calm existence in their New York apartment, a quiet summer stay in a rented Long Island beach cottage, and the establishment, mostly with Marilyn's money, of a farm in Connecticut near the one where Miller had lived with his first wife.

But there was also a painful ectopic pregnancy, followed by more than one dangerous overdose of sleeping pills from which Miller had to rescue her, and the beginning of his long slide into a caretaking role that required cajoling, scheduling, explaining, worrying about Marilyn's pill-taking habits, and supplying emotional support. In a world that equates womanliness with dependency on a man, he might be forgiven for finding Marilyn's extreme dependency extremely appealing—but now he was paying the price.

When Lena Pepitone joined their New York household as a personal maid to help with

Marilyn's wardrobe, she saw two people who were so polarized that Miller rarely emerged from his study or ate meals with his wife. Marilyn's schedule of sleeping late, acting lessons, and psychiatrist's appointments seemed to exist on a separate planet. Even their going together to a movie was treated by Marilyn as a rare and cherished treat.

Her extreme disorganization and sensitivity must have been hard to take: she was almost always late, drank Bloody Marys for breakfast, sipped champagne the rest of the day, and felt hurt if Miller's parents came to dinner and spoke Yiddish in her presence (being left out of conversations at the dinner table, Marilyn explained to Lena, made her feel like Norma Jeane again, the foster child who was an outsider in other people's families). On the other hand, Arthur Miller's emotional distance and routine of isolated work or hardy country weekends must have seemed dull and difficult to her, too. Even their rare parties betrayed their differences. Marilyn loved to dance, as Norman Rosten and many others have recorded, but Rosten observed that Miller required "a few drinks" before he even attempted "an eerie loping foxtrot, perilously off-balance." In *Strawhead*, the 1986 "memory play" that Norman Mailer wrote about Marilyn as another evidence of his obsession, he ridicules Arthur Miller's failure to make a pass at Marilyn when they first met in 1950 (Marilyn herself seems to have appreciated Miller's attitude), but he does seem closer to the mark when he portrays Miller as a pipe-smoking, slightly boring country squire, and gives him such imaginary lines of dialogue as: "Nothing like taking a bath in water that comes through pipes you threaded yourself."

Norma Jeane, the child who had dreamed of beautiful colors, who longed for gaiety and music, had chosen a father instead of a partner. She had married a worthy man who loved contemplative silence and lived in a world of black and white.

For all Miller's worthiness, and for all his impossible burden of shoring up Marilyn's weak identity, he could be amazingly insensitive, too. There is a glimpse of that in his reply to Fred Guiles, one of Marilyn's more careful biographers. When Guiles asked Miller if Marilyn's final depression might have been partly due to the fact that Inge Morath Miller, his new wife, was about to give birth—after all, Marilyn herself had been depressed and attempted suicide once because of her own inability to "complete" their marriage by bearing a child—Miller dismissed that idea as a "red herring." "She knew I was a father before; she knew the children," Miller replied. "She knew it wasn't anything wrong with me that kept us from having children."

Perhaps the simplest explanation of the end of their marriage came from Dr. Ralph Greenson, who interviewed Arthur Miller when he first took Marilyn as a patient. Dr. Greenson found in him "the attitude of a father who had done more than most fathers would do, and is rapidly coming to the end of his rope."

Greenson advised Miller that his wife needed unconditional love and devotion, that anything less was unbearable to her. But the advice was impossible to follow, or too late, or both. Marilyn turned to Yves Montand, her costar of that period, for the attention and reward of a new affair. Arthur Miller turned more and more inside himself. By the time *The Misfits*, his writer's gift to her, was being filmed, they were emotionally and physically separate. The marriage had lasted slightly more than four years.

Two of Marilyn's patterns during those years were with her long before the marriage and long after it: her compulsive use of sex as a way of getting childlike warmth and nurturing, and her inability to find much adult pleasure or sexual satisfaction for herself. Though her marriage to Miller may have been her most supportive relationship with a man, both personally and professionally, it didn't change the past of the neglected Norma Jeane. Even on her honeymoon in London, she may have had an affair with a photographer, and later, she certainly turned even more desperately to Montand. Dr. Greenson's notes conclude that Marilyn "found it difficult to sustain a series of orgasms with the same individual." That incompleteness could have been the reason why Greenson believed that Marilyn feared and yet was drawn into "situations with homosexual coloring." Perhaps. But by her own testimony, she didn't find sexual satisfaction in affairs with either men or women. Her sexual value to men was the only value she was sure of. By exciting and arousing, she could turn herself from the invisible, unworthy Norma Jeane into the visible, worthwhile Marilyn. She could have some impact, some power, some proof she was alive. The very compulsion to do that seems to have kept her from accepting her real self enough to find sexual pleasure of her own.

Marilyn kept hoping that a relationship with a man would give her the identity she lacked, and that her appearance would give her the man. This impossible search was rewarded and exaggerated by a society that encourages women to get their identity from men—and encourages men to value women for appearance, not mind or heart.

But Marilyn's underlying pattern was also a classic one of the neglected child, male or female. Dr. Hugh Missildine had never met Marilyn when he wrote his classic essay on neglect. "If you suffered from neglect in childhood," he explained, "it may cause you to go from one person to another, hoping that someone will supply whatever is missing. You may not be able to care much about yourself, and think marriage will end this, and then find yourself in the alarming situation of being married but emotionally unattached. . . . Moreover, the person who had neglect in his background is always restless and anxious because he cannot obtain emotional satisfaction. . . . These restless, impulsive moves help to create the illusion of living emotionally. . . . Such a person may, for example, be engaged to be married to one person and simultaneously be maintaining sexual relationships with two or three others. Anyone who offers admiration and respect has appeal to them—and because their need for affection is so great, their ability to discriminate is severely impaired."

This is very much the woman who had other affairs during the courtships with both husbands, even though she loved them; whose affairs became more numerous when her work offered fewer rewards; who exchanged sex for kindness and friendship.

One lifetime friend, Robert Slatzer, even claims that he and Marilyn were married during a quick trip to Mexico and divorced immediately afterward—and that was during her courtship with DiMaggio.

"What is missing," wrote Missildine, "is the continuing opportunity for the child to form and maintain a close, approving attachment with a parent who makes the child feel he is a 'special,' unique and worthy individual."

Perhaps Norma Jeane's neglect started too early and was too complete. Perhaps Marilyn could not have gone back and accepted the child inside herself. But as a woman, she was rarely rewarded for being adult or independent, and often rewarded for being childlike, dependent, "feminine." As an actress, she was applauded for portraying helplessness, innocence, incompetence. She was even rewarded for constantly seeking fatherly men as lovers. In *Let's Make Love* with Yves Montand, critics raved over her sensual performance of Cole Porter's "My Heart Belongs to Daddy," just as they had once approved her "Every Baby Needs a Da Da Daddy" at the beginning of her career. (Can we imagine a male movie star being praised for acting helpless, looking for motherly sex partners, and singing sensuously, "My Heart Belongs to Mommy"?) Because she was a woman Marilyn was encouraged to remain a child.

Toward the end, she lost even the acting that allowed her a reward for playing the child-woman role. She lost the work for which she had learned mannerisms so extreme they were almost those of a female impersonator. She was a thirty-six-year-old woman who feared she had no future, who had no man to give her even the illusion of identity, and who felt like a failure as a woman for not having a child. In that state of weakness, she faced the glamour and strength of the Kennedy men.

Jack Kennedy and Marilyn Monroe probably had met long before his election to the presidency. As early as 1951, there are memories of both the young senator and the starlet attending Hollywood parties given by Charles Feldman, who was Kennedy's frequent host and Marilyn's agent. During the waning months of Marilyn's marriage to Joe DiMaggio, two of her friends claim that she was going out with Kennedy. One of these friends saw them together at a Malibu bar.

Whether those dates were sexual or not, they probably didn't have great meaning, even to Marilyn. This promising young politician had married the year before, and his wife was Jacqueline Bouvier, exactly the kind of beautiful and well-educated woman to whom Marilyn would have felt most inferior. He had a reputation for being sexually—but *only* sexually—interested in other women. In the famous phrase of Nancy Dickerson, who went out with the bachelor Kennedy before she became a distinguished reporter: "Sex to Jack Kennedy was like another cup of coffee, or maybe dessert." In other words, Kennedy was neither someone in Marilyn's world who could help with her career, nor was he the sort of man she turned to as father and protector.

Another version of Jack Kennedy and Marilyn's first encounter is given by Deborah Gould, the third wife of Peter Lawford. Lawford had married Jack's sister Pat in 1954. "Peter told me that Jack—he always called him Jack—had always wanted to meet Marilyn Monroe," Gould said. "It was one of his fantasies. Could Peter arrange for that? He did—he would do anything he was asked to do." That would have been before Kennedy became president, in 1960, and Lawford said the affair continued afterward.

By early 1960, Marilyn was emerging from her marriage to Arthur Miller and feeling rejected because of the one-sided nature of her affair with Yves Montand. That was exactly the time that Kennedy's campaign was getting under way. Here was a powerful, handsome man who had connections to people she knew both in New York and Hollywood, and who also stood for civil rights, a less warlike attitude toward the Soviets, and many of the other issues she instinctively cared about. She was seen at the Lawford beach house at campaign meetings and parties. In spite of her moods, insomnia, and insecurity, a Kennedy political strategist interviewed by Anthony Summers remembered Marilyn as functioning well with that group of a dozen or so that included Jack Kennedy. "They were very close friends," the aide, Pete Summers, recalled years later. "I would say she was a very special guest—the president was really very, very fond of Marilyn. She was delightful, a little bit nervous perhaps, but I think the nervousness was because she was in new territory with people who were political animals. She wasn't totally at ease. I did feel that she was so impressed by Kennedy's charm and charisma that she was almost starry-eyed. . . . But she was totally able to hold her own conversationally; she was very bright."

As July and the Democratic convention in Los Angeles neared, rumors of an affair between Marilyn and Jack Kennedy grew widespread enough to cause Freddy Karger to be "appalled" and to refuse to book his band at a convention ball, which Jack Kennedy planned to attend. According to Marilyn, and to a bartender who saw them together, Marilyn also met Kennedy after his "New Frontier" speech at the end of a convention that had made him

its Democratic presidential nominee. She was not the only woman around whom such Kennedy rumors swirled, but she did seem both secretive about Kennedy and fiercely protective when he was criticized. That was true even at a time when she was despondent over the end of her marriage to Arthur Miller and her own problems were engulfing her.

The idea of an affair between them was public enough that in November, just after Kennedy's election, humorist Art Buchwald wrote in his *Washington Post* column:

Let's Be Firm on Monroe Doctrine

Who will be the next ambassador to Monroe? This is one of the many problems which President-elect Kennedy will have to work on in January. Obviously you can't leave Monroe adrift. There are too many greedy people eyeing her, and now that Ambassador Miller has left she could flounder around without any direction.

If Buchwald was assuming that Jack Kennedy would have to change his ways once he was in the White House, he was wrong. Some women friends continued to meet him at the Carlyle Hotel in New York, the Peter Lawford beach house at Santa Monica, and even the White House. Marilyn was never said to have been at the White House itself, but there were witnesses who saw her at the Carlyle and other places being visited by the president. Accurately or not, Marilyn confided to a few friends the problems of seeing a man who was constantly surrounded with Secret Service agents and who had little time for the preliminaries of lovemaking, but she was exhilarated by what she hinted was a very intimate knowledge of this important and admired leader. She admired him, too. Whatever else may or may not have been going on, one can imagine Marilyn making President Kennedy laugh, and his making Marilyn feel important and serious—a fair and friendly exchange.

But the exchange was far from equal. With her work becoming more fearsome to her, and without a male anchor in her life, Marilyn was very needy and insecure. Whatever magic and childlike allure she may have brought to the cigar smoke and realism of political fund raisers and Kennedy dinners, she was far more replaceable for them than they were for her. Without a call from Pat and Peter Lawford for a dinner at their beach house in Santa Monica, without an invitation to presidential events, Marilyn would have felt—and sometimes been—alone.

But another member of the Kennedy family began to engage her interest. Jeanne Carmen, the actress who was Marilyn's neighbor on Doheny Drive, remembered opening the door of Marilyn's apartment in the summer or fall of 1961 and finding a surprised Robert Kennedy. "He had that expression of not knowing whether to run, walk, or stay," explained Carmen. "I was stunned, and I kept saying, 'Come in,' but went on standing in his way. Finally, Marilyn came flying out of the bathroom . . . she kissed him openly, which was out of character for her. . . ." Jeanne Carmen hadn't been prepared for this. Marilyn had talked of seeing Jack Kennedy, not Bobby. But the shy awkwardness of this younger brother, his sympathy for the underdog, and his special connection with children, may have made him seem far more protective and appealing to Marilyn. The self-contained and sophisticated president was far from the people Marilyn had grown up with, but Bobby's style was oddly working class. And, of all the Kennedy brothers, Bobby had the least reputation for womanizing (though his biographer, Arthur Schlesinger, also pointed out, "Bobby was human. He liked a drink and he liked young women. He indulged that liking when he traveled—and he had to travel a great deal"). Bobby was within a year of Marilyn's age, but he had been married for more than a decade, had seven children, and had recently been named America's Father of the Year. He, not Jack, became the focus of Marilyn's fantasies.

"Her affair with the attorney general would turn out to be much more serious than Marilyn's fling with the President," as one of Marilyn's major biographers, Fred Guiles, explained. "She was not drawn to Bobby physically, as he was to her. But he took a personal interest in her, while the President did not. This was far more dangerous to Marilyn than a strictly sexual attraction would have been."

Bobby and Marilyn were rarely seen in public together, but when they were, there seemed to be some real connection. A New York film director remembered passing them at a party, and hearing a simple exchange from one to the other: "I like you." "I like you, too." Marilyn began to take notes in a small red book, as she explained to Bob Slatzer: "Because Bobby liked to talk about political things. He got mad at me one day because he said I didn't remember anything he told me." Anthony Summers, whose 1985 biography of Marilyn contains the best reporting on this period, quotes Peter Dye, a friend of the Lawfords who was present at their dinners with Bobby and Marilyn. He thought "there was certainly an affair. . . . She was star-struck over him. . . . I think she was turned on by the idea of mental genius. She liked the type, instead of being pushed around like a piece of meat. She was trying to get away from that." Lena Pepitone told Summers of hour-long phone calls from Bobby Kennedy to Marilyn. So did her studio maid, Hazel Washington. Jeanne Carmen recounted an episode in which the two of them, Jeanne and Marilyn, dressed Bobby up in a false beard that belonged to Jack Benny, a baseball cap, and sunglasses, and dared him to go to a nearby nudist beach. In that getup, at that beach, they guaranteed him he wouldn't be recognized. Even Marilyn had never been caught when she had gone to the same beach with a black wig over her blonde hair. Bobby couldn't resist the dare. "We walked up and down, and sat on a blanket we brought from the car," Carmen remembered. "Once we got out there

we found nobody cared. Here were two famous people that nobody recognized—we just sort of lounged around. On the way back, we really laughed a lot."

Others to whom Summers spoke were equally honest but urged caution in making sexual assumptions about the Kennedys and Marilyn. Jeanne Martin, who was then married to Dean Martin, had sometimes seen Marilyn at the Lawfords' beach house, and was "quite sure" that Marilyn had an affair with both Robert and John Kennedy. But, she added, "Unless you're in the bedroom, it's unfair to presume."

Whatever the nature and seriousness of this friendship, other members of the Kennedy family knew about and accepted the new connection between Marilyn and Bobby. After Marilyn's death, this handwritten note on stationery from the Kennedy home in Florida was found among Marilyn's papers:

> Dear Marilyn—
>
> Mother asked me to write and thank you for your sweet note to Daddy—
> He really enjoyed it and you were very cute to send it—
>   Understand that you and Bobby are the new item! We all think you should come with him when he comes back East!
>   Again, thanks for the note—
>
> Love,
Jean Smith

Jean Smith, a Kennedy sister, told Summers through her husband, Stephen Smith, that she had "no recollection" of writing such a letter, but she didn't really deny it. Though the note was undated, it might relate to Joe Kennedy and his stroke in December 1961, which would support other reports that Marilyn and Bobby had begun to see each other before that time. After all, the Kennedy family was one in which the men had public affairs as well as public marriages. It was not only part of a bargain in which divorce was unacceptable; but almost a family imperative (as Jack Kennedy once told Clare Boothe Luce, "Dad told all the boys to get laid as often as possible"). When Pat Lawford had seated a dinner in her home in early 1961, she put Bobby between Marilyn and Kim Novak, for his evident amusement. Preserving marriages and keeping the men entertained seemed to be a bargain that the women accepted, and one for which they had been trained by the many affairs of their father, Joseph Kennedy, who once took his wife, Rose, and his mistress, Gloria Swanson, to Europe on the same boat.

But the Marilyn who was always looking for a family may have mistaken this easy acceptance for a possibility of joining the Kennedys in a very different way. Certainly she was looking for a new man to anchor her drifting life. In the summer of 1961, she had told Lena Pepitone that she hoped to marry Frank Sinatra, with whom she was then having an affair. A few months later she was very upset by his brief engagement to Juliet Prowse. Soon Marilyn began to hint that she might marry again, this time a very important man in government. Friends who assumed she meant Bobby Kennedy were stunned by both her lack of discretion and her lack of realism.

On May 19, 1962, there was to be a "Birthday Salute" to President Kennedy at Madison Square Garden in New York. Though it featured singers from Ella Fitzgerald to Maria Callas, Peter Lawford had the idea of Marilyn Monroe singing "Happy Birthday" to the president—perhaps as a kind of in-joke on his famous brother-in-law. Marilyn was flattered, but also very scared. She was less and less able to perform even short pieces of dialogue for *Something's Got to Give*. She was more and more dependent on pills, on trips to her psychiatrist, and on fantasies. She was so frightened that Joan Greenson, the daughter of her psychiatrist, gave Marilyn the children's book *The Little Engine That Could*, and Marilyn took it with her for confidence. In a transparent dress she had to be sewn into, with a psyche held together with a children's book, pills, and champagne, Marilyn managed a brief, breathy, sexy rendition of "Thanks, Mr. President" (special lyrics had been written to the tune of "Thanks for the Memory"), and then led the crowd in a chorus of "Happy Birthday."

Sitting in the presidential box, his feet on the railing and a cigar in his hand, President Kennedy seemed to enjoy all this immensely. "I can now retire from politics after having had, ah, 'Happy Birthday' sung to me in such a sweet, wholesome way," he said. It was a moment both of great vitality, with the crowd going crazy, and one of great embarrassment. Marilyn's very fear and doped slowness had created long sexy pauses. Her voluptuous body was exposed, but her mind seemed to have receded, as Arthur Schlesinger wrote later, "into her own glittering mist."

"There was something at once magical and desperate about her," Schlesinger explained. "Robert Kennedy, with his curiosity, his sympathy, his absolute directness of response to distress, in some way got through the glittering mist as few did." It was the bow of an honest historian to what had become a public but ambiguous liaison.

Under an assumed name, as Schlesinger also records in his biography of Robert Kennedy, Marilyn had been calling Bobby at his attorney general's office in the Justice Department. Now that police notes on Marilyn's telephone calls from her house in Los Angeles have resurfaced (according to Milo Speriglio, a private detective who devoted years to investigating Marilyn's death, they had been kept privately by the Los Angeles chief of police), there is confirmation that Marilyn had been using a private line and that after June 25, she began calling the general switchboard instead. The discontinuing of that private number is mute testimony to Bobby's need to end this friendship, or affair, or both. The continuing calls to the regular number are just one evidence of Marilyn's desperate efforts to hang on.

Given the political scandal of the Monroe-Kennedy connection, the social climate of the times, and Marilyn's own undependable state of mind, a fair question is: Why hadn't this end come earlier? There is some answer in the Kennedy family tradition that seemed to take relationships with women for granted, and to count as scandal only the breakup of a marriage. There is also some historical precedent for the Kennedy feelings of invulnerability in the White House. President Roosevelt's long affair with Lucy Mercer wasn't written about until after his death. When Eisenhower brought his mistress, Kay Summersby, from London, he relied on the self-restraint of the press. In pre-Watergate, pre–sexual revolution times, such stories just weren't written. The Kennedys may have been more devoted to the sexual double standard than the men who had preceded them, but they weren't different in kind.

Given this real or assumed invulnerability, Marilyn's fascination with the Kennedys, and some honest friendship, especially between Marilyn and Bobby, an equally important question is: Why did this end so abruptly or at all?

The answer ought to include Marilyn's own extreme vulnerability—and perhaps it did. But the real pressure seems to have come from organized crime. Key mob figures were angry at the Justice Department's campaign against them, led by Attorney General Robert Kennedy, and they were threatening to expose the Kennedys. The FBI became increasingly aware of the threats, and their increasing vehemence as mob leaders felt more pressure. Just the day before President Kennedy's Birthday Salute, Jimmy Hoffa, the head of the Mafia-influenced Teamsters Union, had been indicted for extortion. (Bobby may not have known it yet, but subsequent investigations showed that Hoffa actually discussed shooting the attorney general with a high-powered rifle as he rode in an open convertible. "But I'm leery of it," Hoffa reportedly cautioned, "it's too obvious. . . .") Mafia boss Sam Giancana, who was literally threatening to "tell all," was a close friend of Marilyn's lover Frank Sinatra. Even a movie to be made from *The Enemy Within*, the book Robert Kennedy wrote as an exposé of organized crime and the Teamsters, was causing anonymous letters and threats of exposure.

Both the president and the attorney general had ignored J. Edgar Hoover's warnings about their vulnerability to sexual scandal in the past, but they were now forced to look at the peril. Marilyn was one part of this. She was a threat by her own indiscreet and out-of-control presence. She was also a threat because of her intimacy with Sinatra and her visits to the Cal-Neva Lodge in Lake Tahoe, which was frequented and allegedly owned jointly by the mob and Sinatra.

Whatever reasons he gave, Bobby seems to have tried to explain the break-off personally. On June 26, the day after the changing of his private telephone number, Bobby Kennedy came to Los Angeles and Marilyn joined him for dinner at the Lawfords'. On June 27, he drove to Marilyn's house. According to her housekeeper, Bobby stayed about an hour, but

when he left, Marilyn was not "excited by his visit" as she usually was. Indeed, if depression is any measure, such discussions began earlier. Friends and employees alike have testified to Marilyn's deep despair beginning the first few days of June, even before her firing from *Something's Got to Give*.

But in Marilyn's July, one could find an argument for almost any future fate—a cause of depression, or a cheerful sign of a way out. She was still trying desperately and apparently unsuccessfully to reach Bobby. (To Robert Slatzer, she complained that Kennedy "had got what he wanted" and that men "used her only as a plaything.") She was seen disastrously drunk or drugged or both at the Cal-Neva Lodge. She had not yet negotiated her way back into *Something's Got to Give*. On the other hand, Marilyn was making plans for future movies, posing for the photographs in this book, doing interviews with George Barris and others, talking on the phone to friends, and working on her new house. To Slatzer, Marilyn was threatening to have a press conference, or show a notebook, which she kept of some of her conversations with Bobby, to Ethel Kennedy. To Anne Karger, Freddy's mother, she still maintained that she was going to marry Bobby, though Anne tried to say she was deluding herself. To Norman Rosten, whom she phoned in New York, she talked about future plans, a *Life* interview that had just appeared, and a trip East.

As the heat of an August weekend and Marilyn's last days began, Marilyn tried unsuccessfully to reach Robert Kennedy in the San Francisco area where he was staying with Ethel and four of their children. She spent the morning of August 4 with Patricia Newcomb, who had stayed overnight on Friday and inadvertently enraged Marilyn with her ability to sleep late, spent much of the day on the phone to friends, and some time with Dr. Greenson, her psychiatrist. As she frequently did, she probably also took pills containing phenobarbital and chloral hydrate during the day, and phoned her friend Jeanne Carmen several times in an unsuccessful attempt to find still more. As the autopsy would reveal, Marilyn's blood had absorbed about ten times the usually recommended amount of the first chemical, and up to twenty times the usual dose of the second. Friends said that her last phone calls had been more and more slurred in speech, though that was not unusual for Marilyn. The final one had left the phone off the hook and clutched in her hand. Even with her unusual tolerance for drugs, and even without her usual addition of alcohol, she probably breathed her last somewhere before midnight.

From Joe DiMaggio's son to Marlon Brando, friends had called her that day. From her psychiatrist to her housekeeper, she had been surrounded with service. Pat Newcomb had been with her, Jeanne Carmen had talked to her. Sidney Skolsky, her journalist friend who called her each weekend, was told, "Maybe I'll go down to the beach. Everyone's going to be there." That meant the Lawfords, and Marilyn said one of the Kennedys would be there. She did talk on the phone to Peter Lawford, but she stayed home.

In the end, she died alone on a Saturday night.

Organized crime killed Marilyn Monroe. The idea was to frame and discredit the Kennedy administration, thus ending its drive against the Mafia, crime-controlled unions, and other parts of the crime syndicate.

The FBI, CIA, or some right-wing group killed her, with the same motive of framing and discrediting the Kennedys. Why? Because they were too liberal.

The Communist Party or other left-wing elements killed her in order to save Robert Kennedy from exposure—a theory of right-wing groups who opposed the Kennedys.

The Kennedys killed her to avoid the public sex scandal she was threatening.

Those are the theories of conspiracy and murder in descending order of their popularity. Not one can be totally disproved. It's difficult to disprove anything in the negative. But none of the advocates of these theories has dug up enough evidence to make a good journalistic case, much less a legal one.

As for a plot by organized crime, there is this bit of evidence: there were attempts, probably successful, to bug Marilyn Monroe's house, and perhaps the phone lines of the Lawfords as well. Some sources link this effort to the Mafia, though there is at least one allegation that the surveillance was ordered of both Marilyn and the Lawford home by a jealous Joe DiMaggio. Marilyn herself told friends that her house was bugged. In the last months of her life, she carried a purse full of change, and made or received some of her calls in phone booths.

J. Edgar Hoover was not a friend of the Kennedys, or vice versa. But he did seize Marilyn's phone records after her death, thus preventing a personal scandal, and putting the administration in his debt. As for the CIA, many would say that the Kennedys were not critical enough of its operations.

As for the Kennedys, a dead Marilyn was probably more dangerous to them than a live one. They behaved in such a cavalier fashion with Marilyn that it's difficult to believe they feared her. It's even more difficult to believe that Marilyn would have carried through a threat, especially against people whose love and approval she craved. In fact, she had not responded with public accusations against any of the people in her life who had done her harm.

What gives some small credence to all these theories is not that there was a crime. There was a cover-up of a noncrime: the personal relationship between Marilyn and John and Robert Kennedy.

For instance:

It's probable that Robert Kennedy came privately from San Francisco to Los Angeles on Saturday, tried again to explain why Marilyn must stop trying to reach him, spent the evening with the Lawfords or elsewhere, may even have tried to rescue her after her fatal overdose, and was spirited back to San Francisco by air after Marilyn's death.

It's likely that Peter Lawford employed a private detective to sweep the house in the hours after Marilyn's death, and to destroy any evidence embarrassing to the Kennedys, including a suicide note or unfinished letter. Deborah Gould, Lawford's third wife, remembers Lawford confessing such events years later. Marilyn's housekeeper was also seen conscientiously, but oddly, cleaning up even after the arrival of the police.

It's even possible that Marilyn was found still breathing, rushed to Santa Monica Hospital by ambulance in an effort to save her, and returned to her own bed only after she was dead. There is some testimony to this on the part of ambulance drivers from a company that had transported Marilyn before. Anthony Summers reports the possibility that her unsuccessful rescuers could have been Robert Kennedy, or Peter Lawford, or both, responding in alarm to a last slurred phone call from Marilyn.

Events like those would help to explain the five or six hours between the time of Marilyn's probable death and the time the police arrived. They would account for helicopter comings and goings from the Lawford beach house. They would explain the housekeeper's zeal for cleaning. Ironically, this cover-up may have created inconsistencies that were later cited as evidence of murder. In other words, a cover-up of the noncrime of an affair may have led to theories of a crime.

The bottom line is that thorough investigators and tough critics have come up with conclusions like this one in Anthony Summers's *Goddess*: "In all probability, no serious crime was committed that night, although the return of Marilyn's body to her home was highly irregular, and Lawford's destruction of the note clearly unlawful." Aside from this cover-up that, if true, discloses a Robert Kennedy who tried to save Marilyn and then was haunted by the circumstances of her death for the rest of his own life, Summers and most others conclude that Marilyn probably died by her own hand, but not as a clear and conscious suicide. As Diana Trilling wrote just after Marilyn's death, "I think it would be more precise to call this kind of death incidental rather than purposeful—incidental to the desire to escape the pain of living. . . ." In other words, she meant to die for the evening—but not to die forever.

But most tragic of all, the time, effort, and obsession that has gone into explaining Marilyn's death has done little to explain her life. Or her constant brushes with suicide.

If we admit that she died by her own hand, we must also admit that her sugary smile was false, that her external beauty covered intense pain, that this sex goddess, as Andrea Dworkin wrote, "hadn't liked It all along—It—the It they had been doing to her, how many millions of times? . . . her apparent suicide stood at once as accusation and answer: no, Marilyn Monroe, the ideal sexual female, had not liked it."

I daydreamed chiefly about beauty. I dreamed of myself becoming so beautiful that people would turn to look at me when I passed.

—from the unfinished autobiography of Marilyn Monroe

Children who are not the focus of loving attention may come to feel they are invisible. They fight to be noticed to prove they exist.

For Norma Jeane, this feeling of existing only at the periphery of people's vision, of being the center of no one's life, began as early as her consciousness. Talking was not yet a way she could gain attention; and indeed talking to strangers, remembering lines, and just coping with the complexities of language would remain weak points for the rest of her life. Instead, her physical self became and remained her way of proving she was alive. "I never dreamed of anyone loving me as I saw other children loved," Marilyn wrote. "That was too big a stretch for my imagination. I compromised by dreaming of my attracting someone's attention (besides God), of having people look at me and say my name."

For the well-meaning Ida and Albert Bolender, the fundamentalist family with whom Norma Jeane's mother boarded her at birth, nudity was probably not encouraged, even in very young children. Norma Jeane may have discovered early that just taking her clothes off her small body was a gentle form of rebellion that earned notice, but not the razor-strop beatings that might follow such serious misbehavior as upsetting her cereal bowl or taking the tricycle away from the Bolenders' own son.

In fact, Norma Jeane had been rescued as a toddler from one of these beatings by her grandmother, Della Monroe, who lived across the street. Della hated Ida's razor strop and screamed, "Don't ever do that again!" Ida Bolender remembered being so embarrassed that she let Della take her granddaughter to her own house, even though Della—who had recently returned alone after following her third husband all the way to his engineering job in India—was herself in despair and on the edge of breakdown.

For the rest of her life, Marilyn would insist that she remembered waking from a nap in her grandmother's bedroom and "fighting for my life. Something was pressed against my face. It could have been a pillow. I fought with all my strength." There were no other witnesses to any attempt by Della to smother her own granddaughter, and few have trusted Marilyn's memory of an event that would have happened when she was barely more than a year old. But perhaps Della, in her own distress, did believe that only a gentle death could save her daughter's illegitimate child from a life of pain. Just a few days later, Della tried to break through the

Bolenders' door in another rage of rescuing. The police took Della to an asylum. She died there nineteen days later of a heart attack suffered during a manic seizure. Her death would remain a haunting precedent for her daughter, and then for her granddaughter.

Clearly, Norma Jeane could not hope to be rescued by her grandmother, or by her mother, Gladys, who was a semi-stranger she saw only on weekends. To survive, she had to make herself lovable to the Bolenders. Her hunger for attention focused mostly on fantasies of being noticed in the fundamentalist church where the Bolenders went to services twice a week—probably the only place Norma Jeane saw large groups of people.

"No sooner was I in the pew with the organ playing and everyone singing," the grown-up Marilyn remembered of herself as a little girl, "than the impulse would come to me to take off all my clothes. I wanted desperately to stand up naked for God and everyone else to see. I had to clench my teeth and sit on my hands to keep myself from undressing. Sometimes I had to pray hard and beg God to keep me from taking my clothes off.

"My impulse to appear naked and my dreams about it had no shame or sense of sin in them," wrote Marilyn. "Dreaming of people looking at me made me feel less lonely."

When she lived in an orphanage from age nine to age eleven, some nudity was doubtless routine in the girls' dormitory as well as in the gym and showers of the public school nearby. It may have given her a sense both of belonging and of being an individual. "I think I wanted them to see me naked because I was ashamed of the clothes I wore—the never-changing faded blue dress of poverty," Marilyn said, recalling the orphanage uniform, a blue skirt and white blouse. "Naked, I was like other girls and not someone in an orphan's uniform."

This feeling of being more comfortable with nudity than with clothes, especially around women, lasted for most of her life: women friends, housekeepers, even casual acquaintances and employees have all commented on it. As Natasha Lytess, her acting coach and early roommate, wrote about Marilyn: "She'd come wandering naked from her bedroom and into the bathroom. . . . Then—still without a stitch on—Marilyn would drift in a sort of dreamy, sleepwalking daze into the kitchen and fix her own breakfast.

"When she became a famous star," Lytess explained, "Marilyn had her own luxury bungalow on the set, with dressing room, bedroom, wardrobe room, and bathroom.

"And she still ambled unconcerned, completely naked, around her bungalow among wardrobe women, makeup girls, hairdressers.

"Being naked seems to soothe her—almost hypnotize her."

The image of a nude Marilyn Monroe reading, relaxing, or just walking through her own house has been described as titillating or narcissistic by many who have written about her. Indeed, Joe DiMaggio, Marilyn's second and very possessive husband, was angered and confounded by this nonsexual use of nudity, even though only he and one of Marilyn's

women friends might be in the house. But the truth seems much simpler: Marilyn found some odd comfort and sense of being at home with this childhood habit that had brought rare feelings of being alive and belonging to Norma Jeane.

Nonetheless, her nudity in public or around men who were not husbands or lovers was far more purposeful and self-conscious. Even before she was a teenager, she was enjoying and courting the new attention that her developing body brought her, yet there was a sexual motive in it that she didn't share or understand. It made her feel used, even endangered. "I used to lie awake at night wondering why the boys came after me," Marilyn remembered. "I didn't want them that way. I wanted to play games in the street, not in the bedroom. Occasionally, I let one of them kiss me to see if there was anything interesting in the performance. There wasn't.

"I decided finally that the boys came after me because I was an orphan and had no parents to protect me or frighten them off. This decision made me cooler than ever. . . ."

As a young model and actress, this same wariness and self-protectiveness kept her from posing nude or acting in pornographic movies as many other starlets in need of money had done. Her one fifty-dollar nude modeling job—the calendar that was to become the proud possession of millions of men, from garage attendants to J. Edgar Hoover—was done only in desperation for money, after years of refusing better-paying offers to pose nude, and with the flimsy protection of a phony name. But, for most of her life, her dilemma—as well as her art—was revealing enough to achieve the attention she craved, yet not revealing so much that she could be ridiculed or victimized. It is a dilemma this culture imposes on many women whose beauty is their only power.

Intimately with men, Marilyn used her body as a gift, to gain love and approval. In the 1964 production of *After the Fall*, Arthur Miller's autobiographical play in which he portrayed their marriage, Maggie, who is Marilyn, takes her clothes off eagerly in front of her new lover, like a child unwrapping a gift she is eager to give to a parent. By Marilyn's own testimony to her friends, her body was not a source of sexual, orgasmic pleasure to her. By the testimony of lovers, she was often generous, loving, and seeking their approval more than her own pleasure. Sex was less a reward to herself than a price she paid gladly. She was still seeking the love, security, and closeness she had missed as a child.

It was this odd and unchallenging offer of sexual pleasure with only childlike warmth asked in return—of a beautiful adult woman, but one with the frail ego of a neglected child—that made her appeal unique: few could resist the animal magnetism of both a helpless child and a sensuous woman. But for Marilyn, all of her own survival needs to prove she was alive, to be noticed, to belong, to be loved, and to work, depended on her body: her "magic friend," as she described it. Sadly, for anything less than a magic body, the demands were impossible.

From the beginning, Marilyn's vulnerable body was betraying her. Even the normal maturing that brought such pleasurable notice also brought unusual problems.

"Norma Jeane had so much trouble during her menstrual periods, the pain would just about knock her out," Jim Dougherty remembered of his teenage bride. A few years later, as a young model and actress who drove to appointments across the long distances of Los Angeles, she would alarm friends by suddenly pulling her old car off the road, jumping out, and doubling over until the spasm of pain passed. This extreme monthly pain that a few women do suffer—and that only with the feminism of the 1970s became the subject of serious medical research—may have been the initial reason for her reliance on drugs. A reporter who gained entry to her studio dressing room in the 1950s counted fourteen different boxes of prescription pills, apparently all of them given by doctors to numb menstrual pain.

When she was twenty-eight and living in Connecticut, her friend Amy Greene—the wife of photographer Milton Greene, who was helping to form Monroe's film company—insisted on taking Marilyn to a gynecologist friend. The doctor suggested Marilyn consider a hysterectomy. One of Marilyn's doctors has now diagnosed her problem as endometriosis, a condition in which tissue from the uterine lining implants itself outside the uterus, in severe cases like Marilyn's pressing painfully on other organs and nerves. There was also damage from many abortions—some butcheries from her early penniless years, and perhaps later. Abortion did not become legal and safe until eleven years after Marilyn's death. Marilyn, however, refused the idea of a hysterectomy. Childbearing was still something that a woman was either not whole or not marriageable without. "Marilyn was emphatic," Amy Greene remembered. "She said, 'I can't do that. I want to have a child. I'm going to have a son.' "

That desire for a son may have been a way of making up for the past, as well as a patriarchal proof of womanliness. If Marilyn's confession to at least three women friends was true, her young body had conceived—whether as a result of a second sexual assault or an affair after her first marriage, depending either on Marilyn's account or the friend's memory—and she had borne a son who was then put up for adoption by Grace McKee, Norma Jeane's legal guardian. There is no testimony other than Marilyn's to that birth, but she told the story out of a convincing fear that "God would punish her" for giving up that child—perhaps by making her incapable of having another.

Other than Marilyn's words to friends, and her later physical problems, there is little evidence of her dozen or so illegal abortions. But one can imagine her sacrificing contraception and her own safety to spontaneity, magic, and the sexual satisfaction of the man she was with. During her teenage marriage, she had been so ignorant of her own body that her husband had to help her remove a diaphragm. Later, contraception still required an unromantic preparation, and it's hard to imagine the eager-to-please Norma Jeane asking men to take that responsibility. Marilyn told one of her hairdressers in the mid-1950s that she had tried to solve this dilemma—and the fact that studios rarely hired married starlets, much less those with children—by undergoing a tube-tying operation to be sterilized. A second friend supported that story by remembering that Marilyn said she later had the operation reversed, though that would have been surgically difficult. Whatever the facts of the process, it's clear that a major theme of her life was an exaggerated version of most women's struggles to control their reproductive lives. For Marilyn, this process was further pressured by trying to do what the studio said, or what husbands and lovers wanted.

During her marriage to Arthur Miller, when she finally hoped to be pregnant—indeed, when she talked and planned, publicly and privately, about her great desire to have a child— Marilyn's badly scarred body betrayed her again. One painful ectopic pregnancy had to be ended surgically. A second pregnancy ended in miscarriage. In spite of undergoing a gynecological operation at the age of thirty-three to aid her conceiving, her last rumored pregnancy came too late for the marriage to Miller that she hoped would be completed by a child. It was a pregnancy by a lover, not a husband, and ended in abortion. Her body had conceived only when she herself needed mothering too much to become a mother, or when she would have had to bear a child as fatherless as she herself had been.

There were other surgical operations on this body that was the focus of all her own hopes and millions of public fantasies. As a child, a difficult tonsillectomy had meant lonely time in a hospital ward where she fantasized that her father would save her. As a starlet, she had minor plastic surgery to add cartilage to her jaw and perhaps also to narrow the tip of her nose. Reportedly, other cosmetic procedures were performed at various times. As a twenty-five-year-old star, she underwent an appendectomy and, toward the end of her life, her gallbladder was removed. Including the self-confessed abortions, her body underwent some twenty or more surgical invasions before she died at thirty-six. Perhaps for this reason, she no longer took comfort in nudity or casually revealed her scarred body, even to women friends, in the last months of her life.

She was fearful of doctors. As Amy Greene discovered, Marilyn would not go to the gynecologist's office alone. But, as usual, she often tried to be gay and entertaining in public about her operations. To photographer George Barris, she credited her gallbladder surgery with keeping down the weight that she often gained between films. Ten years earlier, before undergoing an appendectomy, she had taped a surprise hand-scrawled note to her stomach that was uncovered in the operating room: "Most important to Read Before operation:"

Dear Doctor,

Cut as little as possible I know it seems vain but that doesn't really enter into it—the fact that I'm a woman is important and means much to me. Save please (can't ask you enough) what you can—I'm in your hands. You have children and you must know what it means—please Doctor—I know somehow you will! thank you—thank you—for Gods sakes Dear Doctor No ovaries removed—please again do whatever you can to prevent large scars. Thanking you with all my heart.

Marilyn Monroe

But even in the privacy of that operating room, the public's expectations followed her. A nurse wondered aloud whether Marilyn was "blonde all over," as Marilyn herself had once joked to the press. Perhaps in response to the nurse's disillusionment, the bleaching of her pubic hair was later added to her hairdresser's regular ritual of making her acceptably blonde. Lena Pepitone reported that Marilyn also bleached her pubic hair herself, and once burned herself so painfully that she had to stay in bed with ice packs.

And there were other rituals. She slept in a bra in order to preserve the muscle tone of her breasts, and told a woman friend that she put one on immediately after making love. She was often late for appointments because she completely redid her makeup, and even had her hair shampooed and reset several times, in her nervousness that she look exactly right. She stayed soaking in hot perfumed baths long past the time when she was supposed to be out and dressed. As she wrote, "Sometimes I know the truth of what I'm doing. It isn't Marilyn Monroe in the tub but Norma Jeane. . . . She used to have to bathe in water used by six or eight other people. . . . And it seems that Norma can't get enough of fresh bath water that smells of real perfume." She would call friends for reassurance on the smallest details of what to wear, even whether to shampoo her hair; rehearse and write down subjects for conversation; and agonize nervously for hours before any appointment relating to her life as an actress, or even before meeting a new person. Toward the end, a friend reports, Marilyn was also taking hormone shots to retard aging. And always there were the pills in growing numbers: some to sleep, others to wake up when she was groggy from the first ones, more to calm nervousness, still more to stay alert when the hours of lost sleep took their toll. Toward the end, she was also injecting herself with these same prescriptions to speed or increase their effect.

In between, there was champagne, her favorite drink, and her fairly ordinary taste in food. She played off doctors against each other to get more prescriptions or to take drugs in combinations that few would have approved, but her dependencies were also nurtured and encouraged by many movie executives and doctors. Drugs were a fairly routine way of keeping expensive talent working in the Hollywood of the 1950s and early 1960s. If actors and actresses felt they could not function without them, they were often supplied, or even recommended.

In addition to menstrual pain, Lauren Bacall, who worked with Marilyn, remembers that the early Marilyn was the victim of headaches. Natasha Lytess remembers on their first meeting that Marilyn spoke with a constriction of her voice that seemed to come from nerves. In the mid-1950s, Henry Rosenfeld, a New York businessman who knew her from early in her career until her death, described a Marilyn who "came out in red blotches at the

idea of meeting a new acquaintance, such was her fear." Renée Taylor, one of Lee Strasberg's private students, remembered Marilyn putting Calamine lotion on her face to soothe a rash that resulted from nerves—sheer fear of performance. When she was trying to become pregnant, she would have false pregnancies, gaining perhaps fifteen pounds every few months to reinforce the hope that she had conceived. By the time of her last and unfinished film, *Something's Got to Give*, producer Henry Weinstein remembers a Marilyn who was so fearful that, even when she did arrive at the studio, she might stop by the studio gate and throw up before she was able to enter the soundstage. "Very few people experience terror," Weinstein explained. "We all experience anxiety, unhappiness, heartbreaks, but that was sheer primal terror."

The fear of performing might also cause her to pretend to illnesses she didn't have, a habit that lost the sympathy and tried the patience even of her friends. On that last movie set, for instance, Marilyn insisted she had lost her voice. She forgot, chatted animatedly with a friend, and then guiltily went hoarse again when she realized she had betrayed her own deception. Years earlier, while making *River of No Return*, she insisted she had broken her leg, though X rays revealed no such thing and doctors politely suggested "perhaps" a sprain. Her large number of colds, viruses, and other minor illnesses included some that were more refuge than real.

Perhaps, whether consciously or not, Marilyn's hope for comfort through illness was based on a sense memory. When Norma Jeane was a lonely five-year-old living with the Bolenders and came down with whooping cough, her mother moved in with her, nursing her day and night. It was the first and only time in her childhood that she was the center of someone's complete loving attention. It was a moment of rescue she may have longed to achieve again.

Perhaps, too, Marilyn's lifetime trouble with sleeping had origins in that terrified memory of waking up from a nap as a child, fighting to keep from being smothered at the hands of her own depressed and desperate grandmother. The prospect of sleep may have come to include the idea of death—the fear of never waking.

Certainly, the grown-up Norma Jeane continued to neglect herself, just as she had been neglected as a child. She could not break the pattern. Alone, without the public pressure of being Marilyn, she sometimes wouldn't bother to bathe, or wash her hair, or change out of an old bathrobe. She could ignore runs in her stockings, or menstrual stains on her skirt. When the mist of drugs took over, some of this carelessness overlapped into her public life. Singer Eddie Fisher, who was then married to Elizabeth Taylor, remembers Marilyn after her separation from Arthur Miller, at a party at a Nevada gambling casino where Frank Sinatra was performing. "Elizabeth and I sat in the audience," he recalled, "with Dean and Jeanne Martin and Marilyn Monroe, who was having an affair with Sinatra, to watch his act. But all eyes were on Marilyn as she swayed back and forth to the music and pounded her hands on the stage, her breasts falling out of her low-cut dress. She was so beautiful and so drunk." A few months later, a guest at Peter Lawford's beach house, where Marilyn was often a guest during the last two years of her life, described her sad figure "half doped a lot of the time," oblivious to the spreading bloodstain on her white pants as she lounged on cushions or walked aimlessly on the beach.

The woman who feared most of all becoming a joke, being used or victimized, was succumbing to her greatest fear. Only Norma Jeane would have known the cruel distance between the nightmare of the nonperson she believed herself to be and the dream of the public Marilyn—and that distance was diminishing. She felt "unimportant and insignificant," her last psychiatrist, Dr. Ralph Greenson, explained. "The main mechanism she used to bring some feeling of stability and significance to her life was the attractiveness of her body."

Whenever the public artifice failed and the private Norma Jeane seemed to be her only fate again—when another man she looked to for fathering had abandoned her, when she was criticized or blamed, when she had failed to have a child or otherwise bring reality to her public persona—then depression and hopelessness took over. Marilyn said she had attempted suicide twice before she was nineteen. When she was twenty-four, Natasha Lytess saved her a third time. There were three near-deaths during her marriage to Arthur Miller, and at least two more close calls before the final act.

She was still beautiful and a good actress to the end. The costume tests and outtakes from the unfinished *Something's Got to Give* show a luminescence and magic that her imitators can't capture. Studio executives of that film knew she had just been saved from self-induced death by overdose, accidental or not, but, as one explained callously, "If she'd had a heart attack we'd never get insurance for the production. We don't have that problem. Medically, she's perfectly fit."

And indeed she did appear miraculously free of the usual physical symptoms of addiction. Greenson concluded that, "Although she resembled an addict, she did not seem to be the usual addict." When she occasionally gave up drugs, she apparently did not experience withdrawal. Lee Strasberg, who had taken her into his family in New York, said he tried to help her sleep without pills by giving her the nurturing she had missed as a child. "She wanted to be held," he explained. "Not to be made love to but just to be supported, because when she'd taken the pills they'd somehow react on her so that she would want more. We wouldn't give them to her. That's why she got in the habit of coming over and staying over. I'd hold her a little and she'd go to sleep."

But no one can reach back into the past. Only we can love and accept that child in ourselves, and so have the strength to change the pattern.

Perhaps Marilyn could not have achieved that. Perhaps she had been abandoned too early. But she lived in a time when her body was far more rewarded than the spirit inside. Her body became her prison.

WHO WOULD SHE BE NOW?

*When you're famous you . . . run into human nature
in a raw kind of way. . . . It's nice to be included in
people's fantasies, but you also like to be accepted for your
own sake.*

—Marilyn Monroe

If Marilyn Monroe were alive today, she would have been sixty years old on June 1, 1986. This childlike sex goddess in her sixties is itself a shocking notion.

If we lived through the years of her fame, it forces us to recognize the passage of time in our own lives. If we know her only as a myth, it makes us realize that she was a human being just as perishable as we are. For all of us, imagining Marilyn as she would be today is hard. Her image was so dependent on a sensuous youthfulness that it was bound to self-destruct.

But it would have been much harder for Marilyn. She was terrified of aging. The restriction of her spirit in the airtight prison of beauty was so complete that she literally feared aging more than death itself—not the aging of mind and spirit, which all of us might fear as the loss of our unique selves, but the wrinkling of skin and softening of muscle that changes only the external and most interchangeable part of us.

Even youth was not enough. Nothing can be enough if unreality is the measure. "I'm a failure as a woman," she confided to the head of her movie studio the month before she died. "My men expect so much of me, because of the image they've made of me and that I've made of myself, as a sex symbol. Men expect so much, and I can't live up to it. They expect bells to ring and whistles to whistle, but my anatomy is the same as any other woman's. I can't live up to it."

Clearly, the public Marilyn could never have survived the game without revealing the lost Norma Jeane.

"This sad bitter child who grew up too fast," as Marilyn said, "is hardly ever out of my heart. With success all around me, I can still feel her frightened eyes looking out of mine."

Even such self-destructive behavior as Marilyn's epic lateness made sense when viewed through the eyes of Norma Jeane. "People are waiting for me," explained Marilyn. "People are eager to see me. I'm wanted. And I remember the years I was unwanted. All the hundreds of times nobody wanted to see the little servant girl Norma Jeane—not even her mother."

With enough self-knowledge to recognize her own behavior, but not enough self-

confidence to change it, Marilyn added: "I've tried to change my ways but the things that make me late are too strong—and too pleasing. . . . I feel a queer satisfaction in punishing the people who are wanting me now."

That inner little girl had been created by the mother who was a victim herself; by the father who left his out-of-wedlock child without ever looking back; by foster homes and an orphanage; by that man who, she claimed, sexually attacked her at the age of eight; by all those adults and children alike who treated her as different, an outsider.

Even so, that sad internal Norma Jeane was tenacious. After modeling jobs brought money and approval for her external self, she still tried to keep some real identity. A hairdresser assigned by the modeling agency to bleach and straighten her curly, light-brown hair remembered having to calm her great fears that she would look too "artificial," too different from "the real me." A young photographer who fell in love with her during a modeling trip up the coast discovered that he was really with a shy nineteen-year-old who read her Christian Science prayer book before lunch and refused his gentle, persuasive attempts to get her to pose nude. ("Don't you understand," she told him with her odd mix of shyness and ambition, "I'm going to be a great movie star someday?") Only after she had been traveling for days, insisting on separate rooms, did Norma Jeane let him make love to her. A blizzard produced the storybook situation of two people at a lodge, with only one room available, and Norma Jeane finally gave in.

"She was lovely and very nice," the photographer admitted years later, "but finally it was something she allowed me to do to her."

The shy girl began to disappear inside a created image. Emmeline Snively had warned Norma Jeane that there wasn't "enough upper lip between the end of your nose and your mouth," and suggested she "try smiling with your upper lip drawn down." Remembering this, the new Marilyn practiced in front of the mirror and developed that quivering, self-conscious, improbable smile that was to become a trademark. The studio supplied a new name: "Marilyn" to remind moviegoers of the musical star, Marilyn Miller. "Monroe," her family name, was added to be alliterative Hollywood-style.

Starlets were photographed for endless cheesecake shots. The new Marilyn obliged by posing in everything from bathing suits to well-placed magazine covers. Starlets were also asked to dress up parties and decorate the arms of studio executives. Norma Jeane stood mutely among people much richer and better educated than she—until she could stand it no more. "As soon as I could afford an evening gown," Marilyn remembered, "I bought the loudest one I could find. It was a bright red low-cut dress, and my arrival in it usually infuriated half the women present. I was sorry in a way to do this, but I had a long way to go and I needed a lot of advertising to get there."

In return for help from agents and studio executives, she gave in sexually again. Referring to the variety of lovemaking that men who are old or powerful or fond of degrading women seem to prefer, Marilyn later confessed to her New York friend Amy Greene: "I spent a great deal of time on my knees."

Actresses were supposed to have dramatic but acceptable life histories. That's when Marilyn began her lifelong habit of tailoring the truth. A mother living in a mental institution was shameful (and perhaps didn't express Marilyn's real feeling of being completely orphaned) so she first told interviewers her mother was dead. Illegitimacy was also unacceptable. She simply said her father had been killed in an accident.

A sexy actress is supposed to take great pleasure in sensuality. The new Marilyn developed her trademark voice and suggestive, playful quotes. That kind of sexual pretension became very intimate indeed with faked pleasure to please even her own lovers. "Marilyn must have been frustrated almost all of the time," said one musician who loved her. "I think she [thought] that she was *supposed* to have sex with a man, because that was something she could do, that she could give."

By the time she had become a star, this artificial creation of a woman called Marilyn Monroe had become so complete and so practiced that she could turn it on or off in a minute. Actor Eli Wallach is one of many colleagues who remember her walking down the street completely unnoticed, and then making heads turn in sudden recognition by assuming her famous mannerisms. "I just felt like being Marilyn for a moment," she would explain.

In her later years, she even spoke of herself in the third person in the disconcerting manner of politicians. "Remember, you've got Marilyn Monroe, you've got to use her," she told a scriptwriter on her final and unfinished film.

Like the shy fortune-teller who manipulated the machinery from within the Wizard of Oz, the young Norma Jeane both manipulated and was concealed by the artifice of Marilyn.

Had Marilyn Monroe lived, she still had many plans for that public self. In spite of drugs and depression, in spite of loneliness and a terror of failure that could paralyze her on movie sets, in spite of many near-deaths by overdose before the fatal one, she continued to have meetings and make calls about her professional future.

She hoped to star in a movie on the life of Jean Harlow. She was talking with composer Jule Styne about a musical version of *A Tree Grows in Brooklyn*, which would also star her friend and former lover Frank Sinatra, and with Gene Kelly about another musical to be set during World War I. She had not given up her longtime plan to do the television version of *Rain*, based on the Somerset Maugham story whose heroine is Sadie Thompson, and she was considering the film that later became *What a Way to Go*.

All those were possible plans for the near future—risky in the 1960s for a star who was nearing forty, but still possible. But even those choices were ironic. Maugham's Sadie Thompson was a sexual victim and doomed. Jean Harlow had died before she reached the age Marilyn was then. Her only known long-term idea was included in a *Redbook* interview published shortly before her death. "I'm looking forward to eventually becoming a marvelous—excuse the word marvelous—character actress," she said with her usual combination of ambition and uncertainty. "I think they've left this kind of appeal out of the movies today. The emphasis is on spring love. But people like Will Rogers and Marie Dressler were people who, as soon as you looked at them, you paid attention because you knew: They've lived; they've learned."

Those are brave words, but it's difficult to imagine the later Marilyn with enough personal strength, or enough acting tones beyond her sexual and childlike ones, to convey the lessons of a woman of fifty, much less one of Marie Dressler's age. Even now, with women's acting range and age expanded by the feminism that began in the 1970s, long after Monroe's death, it's hard to imagine a current Marilyn Monroe crossing those boundaries. Could she have made a Shirley MacLaine–like transition to such roles as the mother in *Terms of Endearment*? Could she now be portraying real women in history with any of the strength of Cicely Tyson or Jane Fonda? Might she have followed the example of Shelley Winters, her contemporary

and a roommate when both were starlets, by creating wonderfully frumpy roles, or nurturing new talent and directing plays at the Actors Studio? Could Marilyn have defeated her debilitating addictions and returned to health as Elizabeth Taylor has done? Could she even have found refuge in those few parts that depict aging sex goddesses—roles like those played by Gloria Swanson in *Sunset Boulevard* or Lila Kedrova in *Zorba the Greek*?

To follow the acting paths of MacLaine or Fonda, this woman who could not control her own life would have had to make us believe in the personal power of other women. To become fully an actress, Marilyn should have done entire plays on stage; yet she was often so fearful that she forgot her lines, even in the short scenes that moviemaking allows. To kick her addictions to sleeping pills, tranquilizers, and alcohol would have meant admitting them— and the private terrors that made them necessary. To play herself as an aging sex goddess would have required a cruel self-vision and the willingness to act out the fate she feared most.

"Yes, there was something special about me, and I knew what it was," the young Marilyn had written about her thoughts as both Norma Jeane and Marilyn. "I was the kind of girl they found dead in a hall bedroom with an empty bottle of sleeping pills in her hand."

Marilyn at sixty would have been impossible without allowing Norma Jeane to be seen, without allowing her to grow up to conquer her fears. Who was that young girl in the eyes of people who once knew her?

The photographer who fell in love with a quiet, daydreaming girl on that modeling trip up the coast remembered her talking about moving to New York to study law at Columbia.

Why? Norma Jeane told him she wished to do good for people.

Where did this working-class California girl who never finished high school get the idea of becoming a lawyer in New York, where she had never been? She lived in the 1940s, when only a handful of women were lawyers, and Columbia was considered liberal for taking a tiny quota of them; yet this was a career and a city that lived in Norma Jeane's imagination.

Throughout her life, Marilyn was to disclose many more of these incongruities and surprises.

When she was a twenty-three-year-old starlet described by Groucho Marx as "Mae West, Theda Bara, and Bo-Peep all rolled into one," a photographer was amazed to see her studying her very marked-up copy of *De Humani Corporis Fabrica*, a detailed sixteenth-century study of human anatomy. Paintings of the Titian school that illustrated this study were pinned up in her poor and messy room. Even late in her life, when she was badly abusing her body with prescription drugs and many abortions, she would give friends expert advice on bone and muscle structure.

Along with Albert Schweitzer and Einstein, Abraham Lincoln was her hero. She had written an essay on him in junior high school, and, as the famous Marilyn, she sought out his biographer, Carl Sandburg. Until the end of her life, she displayed a portrait of Lincoln in each place she lived, and usually a copy of the Gettysburg Address as well.

Volumes of Shelley, Whitman, Keats, and Rilke accompanied her on movie sets where she played the classic dumb blonde. So did novels by Thomas Wolfe and James Joyce, and books on history and mysticism. Often the contrast was too much for observers. Jack Paar was sure Marilyn was putting on an "act" when she read Proust. "I fear that beneath the façade of Marilyn, there was only a frightened waitress in a diner," Paar wrote acidly. When Joe Mankiewicz saw her reading Rilke's *Letters to a Young Poet* while waiting to rehearse her famous dumb blonde role in *All About Eve*, he would have been "less taken aback," as he put it, "to come upon Herr Rilke studying a Marilyn Monroe nude calendar." When he asked her who had recommended Rilke, she said, "Nobody. You see, in my whole life, I haven't read

hardly anything at all. I don't know where to begin. So what I do is, every now and then I go into the Pickwick, and just look around. I leaf through some books, and when I read something that interests me . . . So last night, I bought this one. Is that wrong?"

Marilyn might not read a book straight through, but she dipped into a book until she connected with a passage, or until she had a sense of the sincerity of the author. As her third husband, Arthur Miller, has testified, she had an odd ability to absorb the essence of a writer's message.

Whether out of self-deprecation or self-vision, she could laugh along with those who made fun of her intellectual pursuits. At a New York press conference, she announced plans to make better movies, perhaps "one of the parts in *The Brothers Karamazov* by Dostoyevski." When reporters ridiculed her, Marilyn agreed, "Honey, I couldn't spell any of the names I told you."

On the other hand, something in her could rebel against her own image of being more body than mind. When a drama coach told her he felt "sex vibrations" when she read Chekhov, she told him angrily, "I want to be an artist, not . . . a celluloid aphrodisiac." When a well-known astrologer innocently asked if she, as a Gemini, knew she had been born under the same sign as Rosalind Russell, Judy Garland, and Rosemary Clooney, Marilyn looked him straight in the eye and said: "I know nothing of these people. I was born under the same sign as Ralph Waldo Emerson, Queen Victoria, and Walt Whitman."

Her searches after knowledge were arbitrary and without context. It was as if she were shining a small flashlight of curiosity into the dark room of the world.

But she was interested. She exercised judgment and wasn't overreverential. And she never gave up.

Most of her biographers have belittled or ridiculed her efforts at self-education. In the words of Norman Mailer, for instance, "Uneducated (that familiar woe of a beautiful blonde), she was also cultureless. . . ."

And perhaps she was—as Marilyn. Perhaps that intense curiosity was Norma Jeane trying to set herself free.

Who might Norma Jeane be now? There are other clues:

She loved the out-of-doors, was one of the best players on the orphanage softball team, and skied the first time she tried. Had girls been more encouraged in sports— and had Marilyn's tight dresses and helpless mannerisms not immobilized her later on—she might have been an amateur who took great pleasure in athletics. A young

male friend remembered a twenty-year-old Norma Jeane who mastered the difficult art of tandem surfing, and who enjoyed it even in the chilly water of Malibu winters. Yet that healthy, hardy Norma Jeane turned into the sleepless, mincing, pale Marilyn Monroe whose famous sexy walk was said to be aided by wearing very high-heeled shoes, with one heel a quarter-inch lower than the other.

Like many who feel voiceless and victimized themselves, Norma Jeane had a profound empathy with animals. In her experience, they suffered even more than she did. Tippy, the small dog who was the only living thing that belonged to her in childhood, strayed too often into a neighbor's garden. One morning when Norma Jeane was five, she found her dog. It had been killed by the vengeful neighbor. One of the few stories her mother remembered about her own father was his snatching a kitten out of his daughter's hands in a rage, and throwing it against the wall to kill it. Jim Dougherty loved to hunt. It was a source of revulsion to her that he sometimes asked her to clean or cook game. In one terrifying incident, a deer he had shot and put in their car regained consciousness. Norma Jeane pleaded with him, but could not keep him from strangling it.

Given these memories and her own terror of being unprotected, she tried to protect animals. Once she even suggested bringing a cow into the small apartment where she lived with her young husband; all because she couldn't bear to see the animal standing in the rain.

Later, as Marilyn, she usually took pets with her—a dog, or at least a parakeet—wherever she lived. In New York, she went to a park each week where two boys caught pigeons to sell at the market, and paid fifty cents each to set them all free. When Arthur Miller wrote the film script of *The Misfits* and a short story called "Please Don't Kill Anything," he focused on this empathy with all living things. The movie portrayed her as a sad young divorcée who tries to save wild horses from being captured and sold for killing. In the short story, she was a young wife who throws a fisherman's catch back into the sea.

This feeling for animals and nature is one of the few connections between the lives of Norma Jeane and Marilyn. One can imagine their coming together in a devoted sixty-year-old who runs shelters for abandoned animals, or supports wildlife preserves, or simply enjoys living on a ranch where animals are born and raised.

Norma Jeane was shy, introspective, a daydreamer. By all accounts, she could retreat to her own imagination and remain absorbed for hours at a time. It was the habit of a lonely child who makes her own company, but it was also the habit of an artist who imagines abstract scenes of beautiful colors and forms.

When acting coach Lee Strasberg's daughter, Susan, lent her a sketch pad, Marilyn produced surprisingly good drawings with no training. "In one," Susan remembered, "with quick, round lines depicting a feline sensual grace and movement, she had done a self-portrait. The other was of a little Negro girl in a sad-looking dress, one sock falling down around her ankles."

Norma Jeane, the teenage wife, is remembered by her husband as dressing in immaculate white, with a ribbon in her hair; washing her face as many as fifteen times a day; eating healthy foods; and "keeping that tiny apartment clean, grocery shopping. . . . [She] liked to cook."

Years later, Sheilah Graham, a Hollywood reporter, wrote about Marilyn Monroe's marriage to Joe DiMaggio: "You could find Marilyn by following the trail of her stockings, her bra, her handkerchief, and her handbag, all dropped as she went. He was always trying to train her. And he could not. They reached a point where they could not speak without screaming."

And, of course, Marilyn was taking more and more sleeping pills, washing them down with champagne. The girl who found pleasure in health and orderliness never grew into a woman.

Norma Jeane had a special connection with children. When she was left with Jim Dougherty's two small nephews to feed, bathe, and entertain for weeks on end, she took great pleasure in singing songs, reading them the funny papers, and making them feel happy and secure.

But she was clear then that "the thought of having a baby stood my hair on end. I could see it only as myself, another Norma Jeane in an orphanage. Something would happen to me. Jim would wander off. And there would be this little girl in the blue dress and white blouse living in her 'aunt's' home, washing dishes, being last in the bath water on Saturday night."

As Marilyn, she retained her special connection with children. "To understand Marilyn best," Arthur Miller used to say, "you have to see her around children. They love her; her whole approach to life has their kind of simplicity and directness." She

became a sister to the children of many of her friends, and stayed close to her three stepchildren—DiMaggio's son, Miller's son and daughter—long after those marriages were over. Pictures of her stepchildren were found in her bedroom after she died. But as Marilyn, she was convinced she had to give birth to a baby in order to be a real woman.

When she suffered two miscarriages while married to Arthur Miller, the press made much of this anomaly: the sex goddess who could not bear children. Marilyn's efforts to work with children and give money to orphanages were seen only as her desperate longing to have a biological child. But, as her twelve or thirteen abortions testify, she was able to conceive a child, but may have preferred to remain one.

None of her observers or biographers seem to have considered the possibility that she might have needed to nurture the lost little girl inside herself first before giving birth to someone else. Only then would she have the strength and sense of self to nurture other children.

But women are supposed to give birth to others, not themselves. Sadly, Marilyn believed that, too.

A student, lawyer, teacher, artist, mother, grandmother, defender of animals, rancher, homemaker, sportswoman, rescuer of children—all these are futures we can imagine for Norma Jeane. If acting had become an expression of that real self, not an escape from it, one also can imagine the whole woman who was both Norma Jeane and Marilyn becoming a serious actress and wise comedienne who would still be working in her sixties, with more productive years to come.

But Norma Jeane remained the frightened child of the past. And Marilyn remained the unthreatening half-person that sex goddesses are supposed to be.

It is the lost possibilities of Marilyn Monroe that capture our imaginations. It was the lost Norma Jeane, looking out of Marilyn's eyes, who captured our hearts.

Now that more women are declaring our full humanity—now that we are more likely to be valued for our heads and hearts, not just the bodies that house them—we also wonder: Could we have helped Marilyn survive?

There can be no answer.

But most of us, men as well as women, are trying to bridge some distance between our uniqueness and what the world rewards. If we learn from the life of Marilyn Monroe, she will live on in us.

This was the last photograph ever taken of Marilyn Monroe.

Technical Data

The black-and-white photographs were taken with TRI-X (Kodak) film with exposures according to the time of day.

Color photographs were shot with Ektachrome (Kodak) daylight color film, using Nikon's 35 mm and Rolleiflex's 2¼ × 2¼ cameras with a 1.4 lens.

All of the later photographs were taken in June and July of 1962. Film was processed by professional color and black-and-white photo labs in Los Angeles.